CHRISTIAN ETHICS IN SECULAR WORLDS

CHRISTIAN ETHICS IN SECULAR WORLDS

by
Robin Gill

T&T CLARK
EDINBURGH

T & T CLARK
59 GEORGE STREET
EDINBURGH EH2 2LQ
SCOTLAND

First Published 1991

British Library Cataloguing in Publication Data
Gill, Robin
Christian ethics in secular worlds.
1. Christianity. Ethics
I. Title
241
ISBN 0 567 291987

Typeset by Buccleuch Printers Ltd., Hawick
Printed and bound by Page Bros, Norwich

Contents

Preface

If as Christians we are concerned to share our faith more widely and more intelligently, then I believe that we will need to be intellectually bolder. We will need to be far more constructive and proactive, paying greater attention to all three dimensions of applied theology – to theology, to structures, and to ethics.

We will need to pay more attention to theology in the form of apologetics. Too much current theology is either historical theology or ecclesial theology. Too little starts from secular experience and then tries to show that Christian faith might really have something to offer this experience. In a very modest way my next book, *Gifts* (Collins 1992), will attempt to do this. Since it is to be a Lent Book it will necessarily be less technical than most of my other writings. For a theologian working without footnotes or jargon, and testing out material first on one's own congregation, is a risky business! But perhaps in this respect most of us have become too timid.

We will need to pay more attention to church structures. The main part of my research over the next few years is focused upon the empirical phenomenon of church decline. *Competing Convictions* (SCM Press 1989) reported some of my initial findings, particularly on rural church decline. In *The Myth of the Empty Church* (SPCK 1992) I will take this research a step further, presenting extensive data on urban church decline. Beyond that I must test some of the policy options that British churches might adopt to reverse their long-term decline. Rigorous policy-and-action research is long overdue in this area.

And we will need to pay more attention to Christian ethics in secular worlds. This is obviously the theme of the present book. It is meant to be a foretaste of studies to come. Soon I will be launching a series with Cambridge University Press, to be entitled *New Studies in Christian Ethics*. This series is intended to encourage scholars who are equipped to engage in an area of current moral contention in philosophy or the social sciences and yet might show that Christian ethics has something distinctive to offer – either in terms of moral substance or, perhaps more likely, in terms of underlying justifications. I hope eventually to write one of the monographs in the series myself on *Moral Communities* – amplifying hints that occur in this present book.

I am very conscious that all of this research is only possible because of the great generosity of the late Sir William Leech and the five church charities that he has so richly endowed. Without this I would still be tied to undergraduate teaching and administration. I remain profoundly grateful for this wonderful research opportunity.

I am also indebted to many academic colleagues who have helped me with various parts of this book. The Department of Religious Studies at Newcastle, and especially Professor John Sawyer, has been very supportive. Chapter 1 was first delivered as the John Coffin Memorial Lecture (1990) at London University and is still available as a separate publication from Senate House. The Vice-Chancellor, Professor Stewart Sutherland, and Professor Jack Mahoney were both splendid hosts and I was most flattered to be invited to give this lecture at my *Alma Mater*.

Chapter 2 particularly benefited from discussions with colleagues at a conference on theology and sociology at Bristol University and then Chicago, and Chapter 5 from a symposium at Manchester University on the invitation of Professor Anthony Dyson. Professor Roger Pain from Newcastle University was most helpful on the technical side of biotechnology.

Chapter 8 is rather different from the other chapters in that it is a product of a working group. There is a long-established precedent in the group (going back to John Habgood) for publishing its deliverances in this way. I am very grateful to the other members of the group for all of their vital contributions. The membership included Professors Michael Rawlins, John Walker, Frank Farmer, the late Michael Parkin, and initially Peter Baelz, Dr A. Brewis, Mrs V. Bolter, Mr D. Yare, Mr Chris Mearns, Mr S. L. Barron, Miss A. Willis and the highly efficient secretary Mr Terry Teal. Fr Michael O'Dowd was also a valuable member of the group and, together with Dr Alan Suggate of Durham University, most generously gave my complete manuscript a critical reading. I really am very grateful to them both.

Finally, and as always, my love to Jenny. We have identical computers in separate rooms, but we still meet for the coffee breaks.

Introduction

Christian ethics is both exciting and dangerous. Indeed, I believe that it is the most exciting of all of the theological disciplines. It continuously faces fresh challenges, as scientific and technological innovations give rise to new moral dilemmas, and as old issues in new guises re-emerge in response to a constantly changing society. Just when one generation is tempted to imagine that its moral problems are resolved, the next generation discards what it regards as outdated conventions. In a fast-changing world, moral orders soon appear more as moral disorders. Little, it seems, is left unchallenged: almost everything has become contestable.

Herein lies the danger. Because ethical dilemmas arise in so many new and still-developing spheres, and also because moral principles are being continuously challenged in old spheres, the ethicist soon becomes stretched on too many fronts. Enthusiasm for Christian ethics has seldom been greater. Over the last two decades it has become a vibrant discipline and it is welcomed by individuals in many secular areas. Once it might have been difficult to generate ethical discussions amongst doctors, scientists or those in the business world. Today, in contrast, there are more possibilities of dialogue than can be handled by those of us who attempt to be Christian ethicists.

Not the least of our difficulties is acquiring sufficient secular expertise. Perhaps it is the complexities of modern biotechnology which must be negotiated. Or perhaps it is the competing tensions of differing economic theories as they impinge upon the business world. Or perhaps it is the complex tensions of sociological theories as they relate to interpersonal relationships. Or it might be the web of logistic, technical and theoretical difficulties that surround nuclear deterrence. Or even the fast-changing medical and social evidence relating to AIDS. Or the competing socio-psychological theories relating to sexuality. At every stage the Christian ethicist is confronted with formidable complexities.

To give just a small indication of this, I am at present involved in dialogue within my university in three quite different areas. The first of these involves biochemists and geneticists. We found that we had shared interests and ethical concerns about some of the implications of biotechnology. As mentioned already, the Newcastle scientists helped me considerably in the preparation of Chapter 5 in this book – 'Fabricated Man – Twenty Years On'. Discussion of this chapter encouraged us to hold a joint symposium on the ethics of genetic release (since it was this aspect of biotechnology which most directly involved the empirical research work being done at Newcastle). If nothing else, the symposium convinced all of us that it is rare for a range of scientists and educationalists to discuss their work together, let alone to discuss it also with a Christian ethicist. Issues of considerable importance both to scientists themselves and to the public at large were uncovered in the process. So were imposing complexities.

The symposium soon revealed ethical divisions amongst the scientists themselves. Some argued that the issue of genetic release did not involve matters of principle as such. There was rather a problem of public presentation, and the symposium was regarded by some as a useful way of allaying public fears about biotechnology. And there were important technical problems involving risk analysis. However essentially the crucial social dilemmas surrounding the issue of genetic release concerned the study of feasibility, risk assessment and future viability. All of these were of public concern, since they involved the use of public money, a measure of public acceptance, and the long-term requirements of the community at large. However, they were considered to involve few, if any, matters of deep moral contention.

Another group of scientists disagreed. Some of this group were concerned about the more speculative outcomes of bio-technology, such as human cloning, which they believed did raise serious matters of principle. Others were concerned about the socio-political ramifications of genetic release as it is practised already. For instance there was discussion about the effects upon the Third World of genetically improved cereal seed, whereby poor nations, possibly suffering already from the effects of the international debt cycle, become increasingly dependent upon multinational distributors. Others again were concerned to explore the ethical implications of genetic release for the Green Movement and for notions of conservation. Many of these fears were voiced by Paul Ramsey a generation ago and are considered in my assessment of his *Fabricated Man*.

Of course these differences were not finally resolved at the Newcastle symposium. But they were discussed and debated in an interdisciplinary context. By its nature the latter is inevitably demanding, both because it requires experts to avoid jargon wherever possible (experts soon start to feel vulnerable once they do this), and because each one of us had to enter intellectual territories that were unfamiliar to us. Ethicists in this respect are faced with the same difficulties as others. However, they are confronted with the additional problem of attempting to make some sense of the whole discussion. The dangers inherent in this crucial exercise are only too obvious. They are also clearly apparent in Ramsey's pioneer work. I argue in my assessment that some of his ethical judgements depended upon empirical biotechnological data which we now know to be inaccurate. If nothing else, intellectual humility is essential. By entering a secular world of contestable data, the Christian ethicist inevitably risks future refutation.

A second area of dialogue at Newcastle has been in the area of health. For some twenty years there has been an Ethics Working Group on Medical Issues, meeting under the auspices of the Northern Regional Health Authority. The group was established by Ian Ramsey, when Bishop of Durham, and was subsequently chaired by his successor, John Habgood, and then by the Dean of Durham, Peter Baelz. I inherited the chair in 1988. It should not be confused with the ethical monitoring committees now established in hospitals throughout the country. Having no monitoring powers whatsoever, it has acted instead as a distinguished forum for senior doctors, nurses and health administrators to discuss ethical issues, such as confidentiality, at depth.

When I joined the group it was already clear that there was a considerable interest in, and anxiety about, AIDS. Specifically, members of the group were concerned about the ethical issues that arise from AIDS and social policy. We were all familiar with the developing discussion about the pastoral dimensions of AIDS, in which some theologians and churchpeople (in particular my own bishop, Richard Holloway at Edinburgh) have made very significant contributions. We were also aware of an extensive and important literature discussing the ethical rights of individuals affected by the disease. However, we could find comparatively little discussion of the implications of AIDS for the community at large. Believing this to be a crucial, but neglected, area of ethical concern, we have spent the last two years investigating it in a series of meetings and through an extensive literature search. The final report – 'Ethical Implications of AIDS and Social Policy' – that I wrote with help from the group is included at the end of this book.

A third area of dialogue concerns business ethics. Throughout the university world there has recently been a considerable expansion of management and business studies. Some of this expansion has been at the undergraduate level. However, the increasing popularity of the MBA degree (Master of Business Administration) amongst both business and professional groups, has also contributed to the growth of business studies. Of course, technical skills relating to management studies, economics, statistics, and so forth, form the core of business studies degrees. Yet there is also considerable interest in business and management ethics, both in Britain and in the United States, allied to an uncertainty about how the subject should be taught.

A narrowly confessional approach to business ethics might have only limited relevance to a secular world. Christians are not the only group of people to be concerned about the ethics of particular business practices. After the Borsky trial in the United States and the Guinness trial in Britain, there is now widespread concern about some business practices and an interest in the larger implications of viewing the business world in ethical terms. Nevertheless, Christian ethicists have already been heavily involved in business ethics – and none more so in Britain than Professor Jack Mahoney at King's College London. The search for relevant categories and for adequate teaching methods in this important area is particularly active at the moment.

A day spent discussing business and management ethics with those taking the MBA at Newcastle soon revealed similar divisions to those found amongst the scientists. Some immediately saw the relevance of ethics to the business and management worlds. Others remained sceptical. Some quickly recognised the sort of tensions identified in Reinhold Niebuhr's classic *Moral Man and Immoral Society*, whereas others regarded their own corporate responsibilities as tightly delimited and as essentially pragmatic. They mirrored in effect a tension that runs deep in the social sciences between those who aspire to be 'value free' and those who believe that value-judgements are inescapable. I examine this tension at length in Chapter 2.

In all of these debates it is vital that Christian ethicists are as well informed as possible about the substantive issues involved. It is also vital that they do not claim to be experts in all of them. Few things are more irritating for scholars than having academic colleagues from unrelated areas informing them about their technical or (more likely) theoretical errors. By their nature academic disciplines are contentious. It is always possible for the outsider to play one expert off against another. Yet such a facility should not be confused with genuine expertise in an area. In the two disciplines in which I have been trained, namely theology and sociology, I am only too aware that it is possible to miss important contributions and to make claims with conviction which are actually based upon ignorance of these contributions.

Nonetheless, if they are to avoid naiveties, ethicists have no choice but to stray into any number of academic areas which are not properly their own. Precisely because so many areas of human endeavour raise ethical dilemmas, and because experts in other areas are not necessarily ethicists themselves, straying soon becomes a way of life. I can see no respectable alternative. And, having strayed, ethicists have to make choices.

Because academic work is by its nature contentious, there is no neutral path that can be steered through it. Even if overt judgements are avoided, implicit judgements are contained in the very selection of one path in preference to many other possible paths. Focus and selection are themselves not neutral activities.

And even a focus upon current orthodoxies in science ignores the repeated evidence of the history of science that it is some of the present 'heresies' which will become the future 'orthodoxies'. But having reached this conclusion an obvious question arises. Which of the present 'heresies' are those which will one day become 'orthodoxies' and which are those which will simply remain 'heresies'? Theologians should be especially aware of this problem! If I have made empirical or theoretical errors in the papers that follow, I can only apologise. Despite the help of so many colleagues from other disciplines, errors are bound to remain. Christian ethics in secular worlds of incrementing complexities becomes an ever more risky business.

An alternative title for this book might have been *Faith in Ethics*. The ambiguity of that title would certainly have captured something of the double-edged nature of the chapters that follow. Some were written to encourage the notion that ethical reflection, despite the complexities of areas such as bio-technology or AIDS, does matter even in apparently quite secular worlds. Indeed, it is currently a subject of considerable debate amongst sociologists of religion about just how 'secular' society really is today. The sixth chapter – 'The Moral Function of Religion' – will offer a critique of some of the specific claims relating to values that are made in some secularisation theories. However, the term 'secular' can be used without any necessary connotations about a process of 'secularisation'. In this sense, there are important questions to be raised about the role of the Christian ethicist in secular worlds. Those chapters which talk more about values in general and less about specifically Christian values – especially the final one on 'AIDS and Social Policy' – offer one version of this role.

Most of the other chapters offer an alternative, and more explicitly Christian, role. It is these which are reflected in the second meaning present in the title *Faith in Ethics*. Christian ethicists today are rightly paying increasing attention to the faith components that make Christian ethics specifically Christian. I offer a general critique of these in the opening chapter, 'New Directions in Christian Ethics'. It is, I believe, by giving greater attention to the moral communities that give rise to and sustain values that the specific contribution of Christian ethics becomes most apparent. The notion of moral communities also provides a crucial link in my thinking between sociological and theological notions. There are, as I argue in the second chapter – 'Theologians and Sociologists: a Comparison' – some important, and perhaps unexpected, points of contact between the two disciplines. Their varying relationships to value judgements or orientations and to moral communities are particularly crucial.

Recently there has been a considerable revival of interest in ecological issues. The concerns raised in the early 1970s in such documents as *A Blueprint for Survival* and *Sinews for Survival* have returned with a vengeance. Green issues and emerging green theologies are now widely discussed. In Part 2 I will focus upon three of these. In Chapter 3 I will examine in some detail the Church of England's recent report *Faith in the Countryside*. It raises many important issues relating to local ecology and to the role of churches in rural areas. In Chapter 4 I will examine some of the tensions involved in ethical debates about ecology in terms of the concepts of 'progress' and 'survival'. And in Chapter 5 I will examine some of the ethical issues arising from changes that are taking place in biotechnology.

The focus of Part 3 will be upon society. Chapter 6 will examine critically the notion that 'religion' has an overall moral function in society. In Chapter 7 I will return to some of the vexed issues involved in the nuclear debate – albeit focusing here specifically upon recent theological contributions to this debate. And in Chapter 8 I will present the findings of the report on AIDS and social policy.

It is my hope that together these studies might help to deepen our understanding of Christian ethics in secular worlds. In some other areas of theology it *might* be possible to ignore the world around us – although even on this point I am far from convinced. However, in Christian ethics it would be patent nonsense. Whatever the risks and whatever the intellectual difficulties, it is imperative that Christian ethics engages with the world at large in all of its complexities. The secular world is the very *raison d'être* of Christian ethics.

Part 1

Evolving Methods

I

New Directions in Christian Ethics

Twenty-five years ago the two central traditions of Christian ethics in the West suffered a serious loss of nerve. Both the traditional Catholic natural law approach to ethics and the Reformed biblically based approach were showing manifest signs of intellectual weakness. Neither seemed capable of challenging the intellectual rigour of secular moral philosophy or of coping adequately with the evident pluralism that had increasingly characterised the theological world. The crisis in the traditional Catholic world reached a head with *Humanae Vitae* in 1968. The crisis in the Reformed world centred around the New Morality and crystalised intellectually around Joseph Fletcher's *Situation Ethics*, first published in Britain in 1966.

Had Christian ethics virtually disappeared as an intellectual discipline as a result of these crises few might have been surprised. Some secularisation theorists even suggested at the time that this would seem to be inevitable. In the modern world it is rational and bureaucratic procedures that determine moral behaviour, not the supernaturalist resources of various forms of Christian ethics.[1] Even churches should be expected increasingly to depend upon these secular procedures, in effect rendering Christian ethics all but obsolete.

Yet this has not happened. Christian ethics as an intellectual discipline has shown a remarkable resurgence over the last two decades. In most British universities where theology is taught

[1] See Bryan Wilson, *Religion in Secular Society*, Watts 1966, and *Contemporary Transformations of Religion*, OUP 1976. For a critique, see my *Competing Convictions*, SCM Press 1989.

I

Christian ethics is now a major component. Indeed, in a number of departments or faculties it is the most popular honours option and it is spawning an increasing number of the most able postgraduate students. If once biblical studies or systematic theology attracted the best students, whereas Christian ethics, if it was considered at all, was treated as a minor subsidiary (moral hints and tips for ordinands), today the situation is quite different. And whilst Catholic seminaries always did regard moral theology as important (albeit as an exclusively Catholic domain), Anglican theological training only made Christian ethics a requirement after my own training at King's College London.

Just as importantly, books in Christian ethics flourish. We now expect systematic theologians such as John Macquarrie or Jurgen Moltmann to have a serious commitment to Christian ethics. If once it was thought possible to do systematic theology in isolation, treating ethical issues as peripheral, the current emphasis upon praxis makes such an approach appear thoroughly archaic. It appears increasingly anachronistic to imagine that theology can somehow avoid both the influence of society and its own implications for society.[2] If once Christian ethics was regarded as the sub-discipline which applies the insights generously passed down from biblical studies and systematic theology (a sub-discipline in effect for those who are practically minded and rather weak on theory), today there is renewed intellectual vigour apparent in the growing Christian ethics literature.

There is also a growing conviction that Christian ethics is actually at the very heart of Christian theology. Obviously this conviction characterises liberation theology. It is one of the most repeated claims of liberation theologians that adequate theology must start from examining its own relation to society and, in an oppressive society, its own relation to the oppressed. They insist that it is a moral commitment to the poor and oppressed that is a prerequisite of adequate theology. But it is wider than this. Even in social contexts where it is more debatable whether the language of oppressed and oppressors fully applies, there seems

[2] See further, my *Theology and Sociology: A Reader*, Chapman 1987 and Paulist 1988.

to be a growing conviction that moral issues should guide, structure and even judge theology. *Faith in the City*,[3] although not a formally theological document, is thoroughly in tune with this new conviction. Despite theological weaknesses, which I will examine in Chapter 3, it has fostered not only considerable social action in churches but in addition a significant theological debate.[4]

Why has all of this occurred? I don't mean which social sub-groups effected this paradoxical resurgence of Christian ethics (although the influence of liberation theologians is clearly a factor). For once I am not asking a straightforward sociological question. Rather, what intellectual and theological changes might have effected this resurgence?

I

To answer this question it is important to go back to the debates of the 1960s and to isolate some of the broad intellectual changes that seem to have occurred in the meantime. Given the constraints of space it is obviously necessary to generalise. Not all exponents of Christian ethics then or now will fit comfortably into these generalisations. Typologies are but heuristic devices. They are necessarily over schematic and must be superseded as quickly as possible. However for the moment they might help to unravel the seeming paradox of a resurgent Christian ethics arising from the ashes of the Catholic and Reformed approaches of the previous generation.

At a theological level the debate that reached a head with the publication of *Humanae Vitae*[5] was in part a debate about the adequacy of natural law theory in Christian ethics. Doubtless at a cultural level *Humanae Vitae* was a response (a negative response that is) to sexual changes that had been fermenting for most of the century. At an ecclesiastical level it represented a struggle over power and authority, a struggle between Rome and dispersed Catholicism, between a celibate clergy and an increas-ingly educated laity, and between modernist and traditional

[3] *Faith in the City*, The Report of the Archbishop of Canterbury's Commis-sion on Urban Priority Areas, Church House Publishing 1985.

[4] See further, my *Beyond Decline*, SCM Press 1988.

[5] Paul VI's Encyclical Letter *Humanae Vitae*, Catholic Truth Society 1968. For a discussion, see my *A Textbook of Christian Ethics*, T&T Clark 1985.

factions within the Vatican. However, from the perspective of Christian ethics it raised fundamental problems about the adequacy of a traditional understanding of natural law. If *Pacem in Terris*[6] was amongst the last of the encyclicals to be heralded amongst both Catholics and non-Catholics as a triumph of natural law ethics, *Humanae Vitae* was widely dismissed precisely because of its dependence upon natural law in an area (sexuality) in which natural law assumptions were already breaking down in society at large.

At its best natural law ethics was able to give a clear answer to questions about the distinctiveness of Christian ethics. It maintained that there was a clear and rationally demonstrable connection between secular moral reasoning and the most central claims of Christian ethics. The two, if properly understood, could not conflict. Natural law and divine law are continuous: the latter builds upon and adds to the former: divine law never contradicts natural law: grace crowns nature. So, if a secular moralist and a Christian discuss a moral issue they should, unless they are ignorant, prejudiced or perverse, have a common groundwork. Christians should be perfectly happy to use their intelligence to the full on moral issues. There need be no holding back or waiting upon the church to pronounce. Rational enquiry is not an enemy of moral enquiry. On the contrary, it is the very foundation upon which Christian ethics builds, albeit with the added benefit of revelation. Even if pure reason cannot deliver salvation (for that grace is essential), it can at least convict us of the good.

On this understanding, Christian ethics is distinct from secular moral philosophy only because of its additional resource – revelation. It is not distinct in terms of moral reasoning as such. Doubtless disputes will arise between rational people, whether they are Christians or non-Christians. This is only to be expected in a world that is often sinful and ignorant. But such disputes, and the moral pluralism that they reflect and foster, are not in themselves evidence against natural law.

Whilst there was sufficient cultural unanimity, or at least an effective cultural hegemony, this understanding of Christian

---

[6] John XXIII's Encyclical Letter *Pacem in Terris*, Catholic Truth Society 1963. Again, for a discussion, see my *Textbook*.

ethics appeared plausible to its proponents. In a religious enclave, or in a society that publicly reflects a broad consensus on moral issues, it does seem plausible to believe that all right-minded individuals will be able to arrive at similar moral conclusions through the use of their rational powers alone. Doubtless self-interest will tend to distort the moral thinking of many in an area as prone to this as human sexuality. And, of course, it is unfortunate that moral decisions about sexuality have to be made acutely by the young. Yet mature people of reason, such as judges, doctors and the clergy (even when celibate), should be able to think issues through from first principles and reach uniform moral conclusions to instruct the young. In Chapter 6 it will even be seen that similar assumptions prevailed in Basil Mitchell's analysis of the Hart/Devlin debate of the 1960s.

If educated Catholics still believed this in 1968, *Humanae Vitae* proved many of them wrong. It made biological claims about human sexuality which many considered to be mistaken, and then drew moral conclusions from these claims which they believed simply to be wrong. Thus, it was often argued by Catholic opponents of *Humanae Vitae* that unitive and pro-creative elements were frequently separated in spontaneous human sexuality; for example, in the sexual unions of those past child-bearing age or of those of child-bearing age who are spontaneously infertile. Even abortion and masturbation occur spontaneously and therefore presumably naturally, as might homosexuality in the animal kingdom. To regard some things as 'natural' (e.g. medically monitored safe-periods) and therefore as morally allowable and other things as not (e.g. barrier or oral forms of contraception), seemed to owe as much to cultural fashion as to independent reasoning. After all, it was soon remembered, even Aquinas thought that slavery and the rational inferiority of women were 'natural'.

Humanae Vitae represented a watershed. It attempted to maintain Catholic moral consensus in an area which was already profoundly pluralistic. It used natural law arguments in a way which demonstrated more widely than usual the difficulty of making them plausible in this context of pluralism. And it unintentionally promoted active disobedience amongst many Western Catholics. As Jack Mahoney has observed; 'apart from those members who, tragically, left the Church or felt expelled from it, many others took a half step back from it and began perhaps for the first time to take a somewhat more detached view of it than they had hitherto as the entire Church was being forced to examine itself and to follow through the practical and theological implications of events'.[7]

Precisely because *Humanae Vitae* involved issues which few married Catholics could avoid, it forced them to distinguish carefully between what they deemed to be right and what they thought their church deemed to be right. Further, this was not simply a cognitive disobedience (as, say, dissent from some doctrinal point might be). It inescapably involved a decision about practice.

I am not claiming from this that natural law ethics is now impossible. I am fully aware of some of the instructive and subtle ways it continues in Catholic moral theology. Later, in Chapter 4, I will defend the overall sense of continuity between Christian and secular forms of ethics presupposed in natural law ethics. All I am claiming is that *Humanae Vitae* focused, and perhaps provoked, a widespread crisis of confidence in traditional natural law approaches. It was perfectly possible for proponents of such approaches to interpret the 1960s in their own terms: ignorance, prejudice and perversity between them could be used to account for all the various levels of moral pluralism on sexual matters apparent in society. It was indeed possible: unfortunately many found it simply implausible.

A parallel approach to Christian ethics also reached a point of crisis in the 1960s. Amongst Reformed theologians there is a long-standing suspicion of natural law theory. At the root of this suspicion lies the conviction that human beings are far too sinful to have access through individual reason to the good and that the only true path to the good is through Scripture. There are, of course, remnants of natural law theory still present in some of Luther's writings. As an ardent polemicist he was inclined to use almost any type of argument when he was struggling to make a point! Augustine was scarcely different. Nevertheless, the overriding conclusion in Luther is that apart from grace any

[7] John Mahoney, *The Making of Moral Theology: A Study of the Roman Catholic Tradition*, OUP 1987, p. 301.

knowledge of the good actually increases our problems. So the Jewish law, whilst it informed Jews about the good, in no way actually helped them to be good. Being good is simply not possible outside a context of justification by faith in Christ. And in any case the extent of human sinfulness effectively overrides independent moral reasoning and free-will.

When Luther was considering moral issues – as he frequently did – it was often sufficient to show that papal teaching or practice was unscriptural. That is to say, the Pope was considered either to be commending or to be doing things which were not to be found in the Bible or, worse still, which contravened things in the Bible. The principle of *sola scriptura* was never as absolute in Luther's own moral reasoning as it was in his moral refutations, but it was still the primary focus. Christian ethics was fundamentally biblical ethics. The Bible was not one resource amongst others for the Christian (alongside tradition, reason, etc.), it was *the* resource above all others.

Given this position, it is not difficult to see that the extensive biblical criticism that has characterised much Reformed scholarship during this century would eventually prove uncomfortable. As long as a unitary view of the Bible could be upheld or enforced biblically based Christian ethics might prosper. Provided that special status was given to the biblical interpretation of certain key figures – for some Luther himself, for others Calvin – the ambiguities and conflicts of the Bible could be reduced to a minimum. Hermeneutics is not a problem as long as one is oblivious to the crucial role of a canonised interpreter. Luther wrote this or that . . . but he was merely mediating Scripture, not reflecting the circumstances of sixteenth-century middle Europe. He was a pure convector.

But, of course, he was not. And as biblical criticism and especially biblical hermeneutics has developed it has become increasingly evident that he was not. There are obvious biases in Luther's selection of Scripture. Like Augustine he had a particular penchant for Paul (all three, after all, were twice-born Christians with a strong polemical tendency). Like most pre-moderns he cheerfully harmonised the Synoptic Gospels. And like most Christians he treated the Jewish Bible as the Old Testament – prefiguring, predicting, and finally fulfilled by, the

New Testament. By current theological standards he was anti-Semitic, patriarchal, authoritarian and unecumenical!

Naturally all of this is unfair to Luther. How was he to know about present-day biblical hermeneutics, about Synoptic scholarship, about feminist theology, or about theology after the Holocaust? That is not my point. I am talking about ourselves, not about Luther. We have changed theologically in so many different ways that it is difficult not to spot that Luther's mediation of Scripture (or Calvin's, or that of any other historical figure) is anachronistic. Biblically based ethics, if it is to survive, cannot plausibly rely upon some canonical mediator. It must be gleaned from our own interaction with Scripture.

And herein lies the problem which was felt so acutely in the 1960s. Critical biblical scholarship is fissiparous by nature and tends to produce pluralism not consensus. For a while in the 1950s there were hopes that biblical theology might counter this tendency. Its proponents argued that there were certain broad theological themes that ran throughout the Bible, giving it its unity, and providing a firm basis upon which present-day theology and Christian ethics could be built. However, theologians in the 1960s became increasingly sceptical about this whole venture. It did not produce the degree of theological consensus that it intended, nor did it overcome the hermeneutical problems involved in taking holistic views of the Bible. Even the very notion of 'the Bible' has now become a matter of contention. Indeed, anyone who has studied James Dunn's seminal *Unity and Diversity of the New Testament*,[8] Norman Gottwald's *The Hebrew Bible*[9] or E. P. Sanders and Margaret Davies' recent *Studying the Synoptic Gospels*[10] will I think be more impressed by the pluralism generated or unearthed by biblical scholarship than by any unity or consensus. Both the Bible as a whole (a highly questionable phrase) and scholarly approaches to the Bible appear highly pluralistic. Indeed, in the next chapter I will argue that theologians and sociologists increasingly resemble each other in their evident pluralisms. What hope of consensus now?

[8] SCM Press 1977.
[9] Fortress 1987.
[10] SCM Press 1989.

The 1960s were characterised by a number of attempts to overcome this dilemma whilst still keeping within the broad framework of biblically based ethics. Amongst these the writings on ethics of Dietrich Bonhoeffer received renewed attention. Bonhoeffer, for all his moral sensitivity and disillusionment with the German Church, articulated the *reductio ad absurdum* of Luther's approach to Christian ethics. In the opening section of *Ethics* he argued that Christian ethics and moral philosophy are wholly and utterly distinct. Christian ethics is a matter of responding to the call of Christ. Moral philosophy is the sinful attempt by human beings to know the good apart from God: it is an expression of human disunion with God. So apart from Christ there can be no morality. This stark conclusion appears in the opening words of *Ethics*:

> 'The knowledge of good and evil seems to be the aim of all ethical reflection. The first task of Christian ethics is to invalidate this knowledge. In launching this attack on the underlying assumptions of all other ethics, Christian ethics stands so completely alone that it becomes questionable whether there is any purpose in speaking of Christian ethics at all. But if one does so notwithstanding, that can only mean that Christian ethics claims to discuss the origin of the whole problem of ethics, and thus professes to be a critique of all ethics simply as ethics.'[11]

Nor does this seem to be simply a sharp counter-cultural response to Nazi tyranny (he wrote this in 1939 or 1940). His Barcelona address of 1929 expresses very similar ideas.[12] If anything the increasing tensions in the Confessing Church and his prison contacts with secular opponents of Nazism may have somewhat modified his sharp contrast between Christian ethics and moral philosophy. There are hints of this in later parts of *Ethics*.[13] Be that as it may, the sharp divide that he expressed in the passage just quoted does put a very heavy emphasis upon *Christian* ethics and appears to rule out any effective moral communication outside the Christian community.

[11] Dietrich Bonhoeffer, *Ethics*, SCM Press 1978 ed, p. 3.
[12] See Dietrich Bonhoeffer, *No Rusty Swords*, Collins 1965.
[13] See further, my *Textbook*.

Bonhoeffer, like Barth, was a modern theologian. He was fully aware of biblical criticism and his Reformed Christian ethics is not dependent upon biblical literalism or upon canonising Luther's biblical interpretation. It is not biblical texts as such which inform his ethics but 'the call of Christ'.[14] This is always something dynamic. The Bible is naturally used to discern this call but it is not to be identified with it. Just as for Barth the Word was not to be confused with the words of Scripture, so for Bonhoeffer the call of Christ was not to be confused with particular Gospel sayings of Jesus.

But this approach does not avoid the problem of hermeneutics. If anything it exacerbates it. Christians notoriously disagree with each other about their understandings of the call of Christ – as they obviously did in Nazi Germany. For those faced with acute moral decisions there is something infuriatingly elusive about Bonhoeffer's notions in *Ethics*, and the few moral conclusions that he does give (e.g. against abortion) do not seem to follow clearly from his own premises.

Joseph Fletcher's *Situation Ethics*[15] – much influenced by Bonhoeffer – sought to remedy some of these deficiencies. By proposing a single principle, that of *agape* from the New Testament, Fletcher argued that the distinctiveness of Christian ethics could be satisfactorily defended. Christians should share with secularists a disdain for moral laws, for values that are somehow 'out there'. Moral behaviour properly understood is a dynamic venture, bringing uncluttered sensitivity to each and every moral situation and deciding on the basis of only a single principle or precept. At best moral laws are simply moral guides. Once treated as absolutes they undermine the very basis of morality, imposing uniform decisions upon situations that might well be quite different. Situation ethics made the radical demand that all should act as moral agents calculating the morality of each situation afresh.

All of this has many parallels with Bonhoeffer. Where Fletcher differed was in his insistence that it is only the single principle or precept that Christians bring to situations that distinguishes them from non-Christians. For Christians *agape* is determina-

[14] See Dietrich Bonhoeffer, *The Cost of Discipleship*, SCM Press 1978.
[15] SCM Press 1966.

tive: for the secularist it might be 'pleasure' or 'that which is most desired' or something similar.

Situation Ethics dominated discussions of Christian ethics amongst non-Catholic theologians in the late 1960s.[16] Even those who ridiculed its argument still spent considerable energy discussing it. Its deficiencies soon became apparent. New Testament scholars were sceptical about the enormous weight that he put upon *agape*. It is after all not the only moral concept in the New Testament and its demands or nature are by no means clear cut. Ethicists were sceptical about its social applicability. How are we to decide about the morality of nuclear deterrence on the basis of *agape*? And in any case, what about the weak and the downtrodden? Is situation ethics really for them? It might appear rather to be an ethic for the educated middle-classes who can unpack every moral situation *de novo*. Or can they? Perhaps most of us for most of the time behave morally more from convention and from the social pressures of our peers than from any independently established moral convictions. I shall return to this social insight presently.

If *Situation Ethics* intended to resolve a dilemma within Reformed approaches to Christian ethics, it may rather have precipitated its crisis. In this respect it might be seen as the Reformed counterpart to the Catholic *Humanae Vitae*. Both hoped to produce consensus in a theologically troubled environment. In the event both produced massive theological disagreements and contributed to the loss of nerve that I have been seeking to illustrate. So perhaps that should have been that. An end to Christian ethics. But it wasn't. Why not?

2

What this fails to take into account is the subsequent loss of nerve amongst moral philosophers. Alasdair MacIntyre's *After Virtue*[17] is I believe crucial for understanding this third dimension and indeed for understanding the resurgence of Christian ethics. MacIntyre is most unusual in that as a moral philosopher

[16] e.g. see J. C. Bennett's *Storm Over Ethics*, Bethany Press 1967 and Fletcher's own *Moral Responsibility*, SCM Press 1967.
[17] Duckworth 1981.

he combines equally the skills of the philosopher and those of the sociologist. He is never content simply to argue about ideas: he is always conscious that ideas are embedded in social contexts and embodied in practices. Perhaps it is this combination which has made him one of the sharpest critics today of atomised, individualistic moral thinking and of the rationalist presuppositions that underlie so much moral philosophy. They also permeate the Catholic and Reformed approaches to Christian ethics that I have just outlined.

The startling claim of MacIntyre's *After Virtue* is that moral philosophy in our pluralist culture has notably failed to resolve crucial moral dilemmas. Thus he claims:

> 'The most striking feature of contemporary moral utterance is that so much of it is used to express disagreements; and the most striking feature of the debates in which these disagreements are expressed is their interminable character. I do not mean by this just that such debates go on and on and on – although they do – but also that they apparently can find no terminus. There seems to be no rational way of securing moral agreement in our culture.'[18]

He illustrates this claim from a number of areas of current moral debate – just-war and anti-war theories in a nuclear age, the competing demands of pro- and anti-abortionists, and the competing demands of libertarians and those holding a strong theory of social justice. In each of these areas he believes that there is no rational way of securing moral agreement. Of course, one side of each of these debates may prevail at a political level. It is no secret that in Britain at the moment just-war theories of nuclear deterrence and libertarian perspectives upon social welfare prevail. Further the 1968 Abortion Act as yet remains substantially unchanged, despite a succession of parliamentary attempts to modify it. However this is not in itself evidence of a rationally established moral agreement. Governments necessarily take sides on such issues, whether or not there is cultural agreement. And when they change they may or more likely may not have won the rational argument. Rational debates in each of these areas all too quickly descend to assertion and counter-

[18] *After Virtue*, p. 6.

assertion (particularly suited to the adversarial system of parliamentary democracy). There seems to be no way of actually resolving them rationally.

But analytical moral philosophy *does* aim to provide such rational resolution. Indeed, it 'aspires to provide rational principles to which appeal may be made by contending parties with conflicting interests'.[19] Nowhere is this more the case than in the celebrated debate about social justice between John Rawls and Robert Nozick. MacIntyre reviews this debate precisely to show that it well fits his theory of the interminable nature of recent moral disagreements. Far from resolving the debate about social justice in contemporary culture, Rawls and Nozick have demonstrated their irresolvable differences and their common foundation in atomised individualism. So, MacIntyre argues, their priorities are quite simply incompatible and their arguments incommensurable:

> 'Rawls make primary what is in effect a principle of equality with respect to needs. His conception of "the worst off" sector of the community is a conception of those whose needs are gravest in respect of income, wealth and other goods. Nozick makes primary what is a principle of equality with respect to entitlement. For Rawls how those who are now in grave need come to be in grave need is irrelevant; justice is made into a matter of present patterns of distribution to which the past is irrelevant. For Nozick only evidence about what has been legitimately acquired in the past is relevant; present patterns of distribution in themselves must be irrelevant to *justice*.'[20]

I am aware that the debate in moral and political philosophy has moved on since 1981 when *After Virtue* was first published.[21] Some regard Nozick's concept of justice as less rationally defensible than it might have appeared then. Yet at the political level the debate is clearly far from being resolved. The only point that need be taken from MacIntyre is the incompatible and perhaps incommensurable features of the Rawls–Nozick debate. But in addition, MacIntyre claims, both Rawls and Nozick

[19] ibid., p. 246.
[20] ibid., p. 248.
[21] See *Postscript to the Second Edition* of *After Virtue*, 1985, and Alasdair MacIntyre, *Whose Justice? Which Rationality?* Duckworth 1988.

harbour the illusion that such moral issues can be resolved in society through individuals arguing rationally from their own resources and their own resources alone.

After Virtue concludes with a strong hint that moral dilemmas can only finally be resolved satisfactorily in moral communities. Rawls and Nozick both argue 'as though we had been ship-wrecked on an uninhabited island with a group of other individuals, each of whom is a stranger to me and to all the others'.[22] Even the socially conscious Rawls starts his famous account of *Justice* with an individual rational agent 'situated behind a veil of ignorance'.[23] In contrast, MacIntyre holds that the tradition of virtues and the moral communities from which they spring offers a more satisfactory basis for resolving moral disagreements. There are strong hints of religious developments to come in his most recent writings in the much quoted concluding words of *After Virtue*:

> 'What matters at this stage is the construction of local forms of community within which civility and the intellectual and moral life can be sustained through the new dark ages which are already upon us. And if the tradition of the virtues was able to survive the horrors of the last dark ages, we are not entirely without grounds for hope. This time, however, the barbarians are not waiting beyond the frontiers; they have already been governing us for quite some time. And it is our lack of consciousness of this that constitutes part of our predicament. We are waiting not for a Godot, but for another – doubtless very different – St. Benedict.'[24]

This celebrated conclusion to *After Virtue* has been accused of obvious hyperbole. Jeffrey Stout, in particular, argues that it exaggerates differences between the present and the past. Stout does not claim that 'everything is fine, that we should just carry on, confident that because disagreement never goes all the way down, we needn't worry about becoming barbarians. But neither do I think that the evidence . . . gives us reason to conclude that the new dark ages are upon us'.[25]

[22] *After Virtue*, p. 250: see also *Whose Justice? Which Rationality?*, pp. 396f.
[23] John B. Rawls, *A Theory of Justice*, OUP 1973, p. 136.
[24] *After Virtue*, p. 263.
[25] Jeffrey Stout, *Ethics After Babel: The Languages of Morals and Their Discontents*, James Clarke 1988, p. 219.

Furthermore, *After Virtue* remains vague about the relationship between moral communities and religious institutions.
However, MacIntyre collaborated subsequently with the group
of American sociologists, led by Robert Bellah, who produced
the much-discussed *Habits of the Heart*[26] in 1985. This book
continues MacIntyre's attack upon moral individualism and
upholds his central contention that communities are essential for
sustainable moral beliefs. Some of the intellectual and methodological weaknesses of *Habits of the Heart* have by now become
apparent. Stout again argues that its 'Socratic probing gets too
heavy-handed'.[27] In addition, it repeatedly generalises about
present-day American mores, yet admits that it was based on
extended interviews with some 200 predominantly white,
middle-class Americans. And it continues the functionalist
conviction of Bellah, first expressed in his influential work on
civil religion, that underneath the pluralism of American culture
there are continuities of moral belief derived from outwardly
diverse religious institutions.[28] Its simplifications in both
respects should be treated with considerable caution. I shall
return to criticisms of Bellah in Chapters 2 and 6.

Nevertheless, *Habits of the Heart* does at least offer a usable
definition of community which might add flesh to MacIntyre's
analysis. The authors distinguish carefully in theory (although
not always in practice) between 'lifestyle enclaves' on the one
hand and 'communities' on the other. For them 'a lifestyle
enclave is formed by people who share some features of private
life. Members of a lifestyle enclave express their identity through
shared patterns of appearance, consumption, and leisure activities, which often serve to differentiate them sharply from those
with other lifestyles. They are not interdependent, do not act
together politically, and do not share a history'.[29]

---

[26] Robert Bellah, Richard Madsen, William M. Sullivan, Ann Swidler and
Steven M. Tipton, *Habits of the Heart: Middle America Observed*, Hutchinson
1985: see also Bellah, *et. al.*, *Individualism and Commitment in American Life:
Readings on the Themes of Habits of the Heart*, Harper and Row, 1987.
[27] op. cit., p. 199.
[28] See James A. Beckford, *Religion and Advanced Industrial Society*, Unwin
Hyman 1989, pp. 69–70.
[29] *Habits of the Heart*, pp. 333–5.

A community, in contrast, 'is a group of people who are socially interdependent, who participate together in discussion and decision-making, and who share certain practices that both define the community and are nurtured by it. Such a community is not quickly formed. It almost always has a history and so is also a community of memory, defined in part by its past and its memory of its past'.[30]

Once these definitions are added to *After Virtue* its thesis becomes even stronger. It is communities, rather than ephemeral lifestyle enclaves, which are crucial for sustainable moral values.

3

If this overall account of recent Christian ethics and moral philosophy is at all accurate, then the fresh opportunities for Christian ethics today, its current resurgence, and even its possible future directions, may by now be clearer. Christianity has always had a heavy investment in communities, in Bellah's sense of the term, and it may have been very foolish for Christian ethicists to have imagined that an adequate view of ethics could ever be developed without making such communities central. Too much Catholic and Reformed ethics has replicated the myth predominant in analytic moral philosophy that the good can be discerned through individual enquiry alone. Community ethics is quite different. Despite some green myths it holds that values do not simply grow on trees, let alone spring solely from rational enquiry: they are fostered and nurtured in communities, and especially in worshipping communities.

There was the occasional voice even in the 1960s stressing the essentially communal nature of Christian ethics. Paul Lehmann's *Ethics in a Christian Context*[31] was an important and early example. His stress upon *koinonia* and the central role of *koinonia* in Christian moral decision-making was a significant alternative to Fletcher. Like Fletcher he believed that moral decisions were made properly only *in situ*: the two shared a general distrust of moral rules. Yet unlike Fletcher it was the *koinonia*, rather than the individual, which exemplified Christian

[30] ibid.
[31] SCM Press 1963.

ethics and in which the distinctiveness of Christian ethics was apparent.

Lehmann's approach was motivated more by the internal debate in Christian ethics than by a felt failure of the individual paradigm in moral philosophy. And for critics at the time his solution was less than convincing. If Fletcher placed too great a stress upon the distinctiveness of *agape*, then Lehmann seemed to place too great a stress upon *koinonia*. It was only too obvious that just as individual Christians did not always seem to exemplify or abide by *agape*, so actual examples of Christian communities did not accord comfortably with his idealised vision of *koinonia*. Nor was it clear that these *koinonia* were relevant to values more widely in a pluralist society. Christian ethics seemed to be confined to a ghetto: its distinctiveness ensured its isolation. Thus although Lehmann's stress upon community was an important corrective, it hardly solved the problems associated with the distinctiveness of Christian ethics in the Reformed tradition.

To resolve this, I believe that an important distinction must be made. Christian communities are the harbingers rather than the exemplars of Christian values. Of course, they can at times be exemplars of Christian values, but all too often they are sinful and/or socially constrained. The media in a pluralist society are particularly adept at pointing to the way Christian communities do not in fact live up to their own professed values. And it is perhaps vital that the media do so. Christian communities may need to be reminded that they are harbingers of values which they frequently flaunt, misunderstand or just fail to notice. Yet their Scriptures, lections, liturgies, hymns and accumulated sources of long-refined wisdom continue to carry these values despite their own manifest frailties. Worshipping communities act as such moral harbingers, whether they realise this or not, and then spill these values more widely into society at large, again whether they realise this or not. Indeed the very moral judgements so frequently offered by the media of Christian communities may act as an important reminder that Christian values are already scattered in society at large.

Some people have been puzzled about the connection between my two fields of research – on the one hand an empirical project on church decline which is examining in detail nineteenth- and twentieth-century census data, and on the other an abiding interest in theology and Christian ethics as social realities. The connection is, in fact, here. Both fields of my research have a central commitment to worshipping communities – a commitment that will become more apparent in Chapter 3. At an empirical level I am concerned about current levels of church-going in Britain and wish to understand better the demographic and cultural factors that seem to lie behind the long-term institutional decline of most denominations. A book still in preparation will explore these factors in detail.[32] And at a theoretical level I am convinced that a theology which revolves around praxis must take seriously the role of churches as worshipping communities. Churchgoing is not simply church-going; it is corporate worship; and it is corporate worship which gives flesh to Christian symbols, language and stories; and it is these that are the primary harbingers of Christian values even in a pluralist society.

Once we free ourselves from the myth that values can be satisfactorily derived from individual rational inspection (a myth that has had a long innings in the West), then we can start to observe how we really do generate values. As argued a little earlier, most of us for most of the time behave morally more from convention and from the social pressures of our peers than from any independently established moral convictions. Far from regarding this insight as shameful, I believe that it should encourage us to spend more time inspecting the communities that establish conventions and the grounds upon which they do so. On this understanding Christian ethics takes a decidedly sociological turn, since it is indeed the business of sociology to inspect communities and social conventions. If Western philosophy has tended to foster individualism – encouraging the myth that individuals really can create *de novo* their own moral framework – sociology tends to pull in the opposite direction. In the process moral communities become an essential ingredient in understanding moral agents.

Some words of caution are necessary at this stage of my argument. An emphasis upon the crucial role of moral communi-

[32] See my *The Myth of the Empty Church*, SPCK 1992.

ties does not of itself commit Christian ethics to a theory of social determinism. This is an emphasis not a strait-jacket. My contention is that both Christian ethics in the 1960s and moral philosophy more generally were over committed to the idea that values could be derived solely from individual rational inspection. In Fletcher's account of situation ethics this led to the quirky result that debates about moral issues became debates about outrageous paradigms. In order to show that there were no moral rules apart from specific moral situations, Fletcher argued time and again that there were always conceivable exceptions to any moral rule. So notions such as sacrificial adultery or justifications of human cloning in order to have an efficient army were offered as serious examples of Christian ethics. However, it would be just as crude to argue that individual rationality must always be subservient to religious communities. Such is the path to the Inquisition and other horrors of Christian history, as well as to some of the more abrasive features of recent Islamic or Jewish fundamentalism. This emphasis is not a strait-jacket: it is a corrective. Of course, individuals must continue to use their own reason – MacIntyre himself obviously still does. What they should no longer imagine is that this could ever be a sufficient resource for morality.

Again, it is important not to hypostasise Christian communities. Communities are by their nature dynamic. Even the most moribund Christian communities change over time. In the modern world they may be changing faster than ever. In a more ecumenical age Christian communities mutually influence each other and all are influenced by society at large. The growing influence of feminism serves as an obvious example of this process. As a movement it has been developed largely outside the churches. Yet Christian feminists soon noticed resonances within some of the historic resources of Christianity and are now actively contributing perspectives gleaned from these resources to secular feminism. Further Christian feminists manifestly cross denominational boundaries, sometimes having more in common with each other than with patriarchal elements in their own denominations.[33] This example reveals a startling range of interaction: feminism influences Christian communities having

[33] cf. Ann Loades (ed.), *Feminist Theology: A Reader*, SPCK 1990.

been adopted by some within those communities; these communities are then placed under continuing inspection from these Christian feminists; some of the resources of these communities in turn shape feminism; and finally Christian feminism interacts with secular feminism. A process that is happening under our noses gives the lie to the idea that there is anything static or deterministic about stressing the communal nature of morality.

Once this sociological step is taken the moral function of churches becomes more evident. Of course, churches are not the only moral communities in society. There is a long line of French functionalism – through Voltaire, Comte, Durkheim and Sartre – which holds in effect that the phenomenon of religion in some form is essential to the stability of society, whilst at the same time remaining highly sceptical of the theological claims of religion. But in reality the modern world abounds with moral communities that owe little to religion – from delinquent gangs to the strong communities fostered by wars. I will examine claims about the moral function of religion further in Chapter 6.

In contrast to the claims of *Habits of the Heart*, religious institutions in advanced capitalist societies may foster not some overall moral unity (despite differences of opinion on specific issues) but highly diverse moral perspectives, ranging from the most conservative to the most radical. The moral force of recent radical Islam in a context of acquiescent forms of Christianity should be sufficient to convince us of that. Where religious communities differ from their secular counterparts is not in their ability to generate and nurture specific values, but in their grounding in worship. They are thus communities – Jewish, Christian, or Islamic – responding in worship to Another, not communities manufacturing and then maintaining values.

This is perhaps my sharpest point of disagreement with Don Cupitt's *The New Christian Ethics*. I would concede to him the need to see the culture-boundness of Christian communities. Christian ethics has often had a tendency to idealise empirical manifestations of the *koinonia*, and to forget, as Cupitt warns, that moral precepts have all too often simply been 'the moralism of life's winners'.[34] But a context of worship suggests more than

[34] Don Cupitt, *The New Christian Ethics*, SCM Press 1988, p. 35.

his bleak dictum 'we make truth and we make values'[35] seems to allow. It is unlikely that many theists could be content with such a dictum. Whilst it is important to view Christian ethics as a perspective that is indeed creative, it is still consciously carried out in a context of God's creation. By apparently abandoning this latter context Cupitt can naturally make little sense of Christian communities as worshipping communities. Again, I will return to Cupitt's arguments in Chapter 6.

Perhaps it is here that a new rapprochement might be possible between Catholic and Reformed approaches to Christian ethics. If individualistic understandings of natural law are abandoned, a more community-based understanding might still survive. Catholics might then concede to those from a Reformed tradition that it is within a worshipping community that the world as being naturally ordered makes most sense. Unless sin really has wholly corrupted everything, it should still be possible to discern natural morality – but mainly for those already nurtured in moral communities. Outsiders would be encouraged to step inside such communities if for the most part they are to find natural law claims plausible.

In turn, Reformed approaches to Christian ethics might learn to engage more fully with society at large, as Catholic moral theology has long attempted to do. By focusing so exclusively upon specifically Christian resources (notably the Bible) Reformed approaches have sometimes given the impression that they are more interested in promoting counter-cultures. The *koinonia* become embattled havens preserving their internal purity but separated from the world at large. Sectarianism in one form or another has been a besetting weakness of the Reformed world – a weakness that may become increasingly evident as mainline denominations in Britain continue to decline. By becoming essentially more Catholic this weakness could be countered and the task of doing Christian ethics in secular worlds could become a reality.

4

I argued at the outset that typologies are but heuristic devices and that it is important that they should be superseded as quickly

[35] ibid., p. 5.

as possible. The moment has come to do just that. There are, of course, signs that what I am predicting is already happening. Indeed, there are continuous traditions in both Catholic and Reformed approaches to Christian ethics which have always stressed the centrality of community. Furthermore, despite MacIntyre, individualistic moral philosophy, searching for the good outside communities and their moral conventions, is far from dead. For some the hope lingers that there really is a rationally demonstrable basis to ethics just waiting to be discovered.

Stylised overviews of disciplines can never hope to capture their more subtle nuances. Nevertheless I think that it is possible to detect the renewed vigour of Christian ethics mentioned at the beginning. The writings of authors such as Stanley Hauerwas,[36] to which I shall return sometimes critically at several points in this book, represent a vigorous and distinctive approach to Christian ethics.

From a theological perspective moral values are not the *raison d'être* of Christianity. They might be Christianity's most visible connection with Western society. But they do not in themselves constitute the Kingdom of God. Theologically, worship is far more central. However in the new climate – in so far as it really does exist – it might be possible for Christian ethicists to become somewhat more courageous. If communities really are essential to ethics, then churches have long been in the business of fostering communities. And it could just be that worship offers a firmer foundation for communities than anything else. That cannot be offered as *the* reason for worshipping, but it might be a sufficient reason for treating worshipping communities with a new moral seriousness even in apparently secular worlds.

---

[36] See particularly, Stanley Hauerwas' *Vision and Virtue*, Fides 1974, *Character and the Christian Life*, Trinity 1975, *The Peaceable Kingdom*, University of Notre Dame 1983 and SCM Press 1984, *Against the Nations*, Winston Press 1985, and *Suffering Presence*, University of Notre Dame 1986 and T&T Clark 1988.

2

Theologians and Sociologists: a Comparison

My thesis, then, is that Christian values are intimately related to Christian communities. In worship especially Christian communities are harbingers of values in tension which provide the basis of Christian ethics. These values spill over into society at large in ways that are often invisible both to the churches themselves and even to society more generally. Without claiming that these values are necessary for the survival or even coherence of society, they may still affect and shape the quality of society. As a result apparently secular worlds in Britain are often embedded in, or at least deeply influenced by, Christian values. And it is for this reason that the Christian ethicist finds so many opportunities of dialogue in the worlds of medicine, science and business studies.

Now all of this seems to run counter to the traditional view of science and particularly of social science. Surely these are value-free enterprises? Unlike theologians, scientists and social scientists are engaged in the study of empirical realities and are not at all concerned with ethical, let alone theological, considerations.

In later chapters I will discuss such claims in the secular worlds of science. However, in this chapter I will focus very specifically upon sociology, and upon the complex dialogue that has developed over the last two decades between theologians and sociologists. There are many signs here of changes that offer new opportunities for those doing Christian ethics in secular worlds.

Peter Berger's celebrated theological Appendix to *The Sacred*

Canopy[1] well expresses the traditional view-point that sociology and theology are quite separate enterprises. In the Preface to this important book Berger insisted that the sociology of religion must 'rigidly bracket throughout any questions of the ultimate truth or illusion of religious propositions':

> 'There is neither explicit nor implied theology in this argument. The brief comments on possible implications of this perspective for the theologian made in Appendix II are not necessary to the argument and do not logically grow out of it. They were motivated by a personal affection for theologians and their enterprise that need not trouble the theologically uninterested reader of this book.'[2]

Even amongst those theologians who did read the book some apparently never reached Appendix II.[3] If they had they would have been firmly warned against the dangers of any easy dialogue between the two disciplines. Berger argued:

> 'Sociology . . . raises questions for the theologian to the extent that the latter's positions hinge on certain socio-historical presuppositions. For better or for worse, such presuppositions are particularly characteristic of theological thought in the Judaeo-Christian orbit, for reasons that are well known and have to do with the radically historical orientation of the Biblical tradition. The Christian theologian is, therefore, ill-advised if he simply views sociology as an ancillary discipline that will help him (or, more likely, help the practical churchman) to understand certain "external" problems of the social environment in which his Church is located.'[4]

In rather patronising tones Berger then mentioned that 'quasi-sociological research' could be useful to churches at an organisational level. Even market research might be of some marginal use. But the sociology of knowledge as a serious intellectual discipline would prove a dangerous bed-fellow for the theologian. He concluded the Appendix with a warning that

---

[1] Peter L. Berger, *The Sacred Canopy*, Doubleday 1967. In Britain this was published as *The Social Reality of Religion*, Penguin edition 1973. All page references refer to the latter.
[2] ibid., p. 7.
[3] See my *The Social Context of Theology*, Mowbrays 1977.
[4] ibid., p. 184.

a serious conversation between sociologists and theologians 'will require partners, on both sides, with a high degree of openness. In the absence of such partners, silence is by far the better course'.[5]

Of course there was an agenda here. Berger the sociologist *par excellence* had started his academic career as a sociologist in a theological seminary. And Berger at that earlier stage was attracted to Barth. But by 1967 Berger was in a thoroughly sociological environment and had come to reject Barthianism. In the Appendix he specifically rejected the theology contained in his *The Precarious Vision*.[6] His love-hate relationship with the churches – albeit with a continuing interest in theological issues – was also evident as was his disdain for the sort of management or business studies that have now supplanted sociologists in many universities.

However, today sociology is so widely used within critical theology (most dramatically by New Testament scholars) that hybrid pedigrees such as my own may no longer be regarded with such suspicion. It is increasingly obvious to theologians that their discipline is never carried out in a social vacuum, but does have social antecedents, social contexts, and social consequences. As a result most major theology and religious studies departments now have a 'resident sociologist', or at least co-operate with other academics in social science departments. Even quite conservative theological groups no longer assume automatically that sociology is ontologically committed to social reductionism/ determinism.

And amongst sociologists there is perhaps today a greater preparedness to allow that value commitment is not a bar to serious research. On the contrary, sociologists do seem more prepared to acknowledge that they are motivated to do one sort of research rather than another because of their prior commitments and interests. Few might now claim to be 'value free' and many might even regard with suspicion those who do make such claims. Certainly amongst sociologists of religion personal religious commitments or hostilities are more frequently admitted in public than they were even twenty years ago.

[5] ibid., p. 190.
[6] Peter L. Berger, *The Precarious Vision*, Doubleday 1961.

Without becoming confessional apologists (secular or denominational) we are more prepared than before to lay our personal biases open to inspection.

Doubtless a number of individual and social factors have brought about these changes. However there are also grounds for thinking that the two disciplines are actually more similar than was usually recognised in the past – and certainly more similar than one would ever have realised from the Berger Appendix. In this chapter I will attempt to unpack some of these points of similarity. Eight points of convergence, largely unmentioned by Berger at the time, might be isolated:

(1) *Similar Methodological Diversity*

One of the first things that a student learns when crossing the boundary between theology and sociology is that neither discipline is unified. There are strong methodological tensions and conflicts within each and individuals have to chose their own paths through them. Within sociology there are obvious tensions between Marxists and non-Marxists, between Weberians and functionalists, between theoretical and statistical approaches, and between so-called qualitative research and quantitative research (one of the sharpest divisions currently in social science faculties). Within theology there are obvious traditional divides between Catholic, Anglican and Reformed approaches – although today divisions between conservative evangelical and critical theologians, between liberal and radical styles of theology, and between linguistic, theoretical and applied approaches, are probably more significant in universities (and cut across denominations). There are clear theoretical links between some of these divisions (e.g. between Marxist sociology and radical theology). There are also sometimes curious similarities between the moral certainties of some conservative evangelical students in theology and Marxist students in sociology. Even the division between qualitative and quantitative research – evident particularly in the division between those who are computer literate and those who are not – can be found amongst theologians.

Nowhere is this more evident than in Biblical studies. Twenty years ago there certainly was not anything approaching unanimity in this area. Notoriously Biblical scholars disagreed with each other about a whole range of issues. James Dunn's *Unity and Diversity of the New Testament*,[7] first published in 1977, is a very able summary of many of these deep divisions in New Testament scholarship. Yet, even as recently as that, he was still able to argue that there were indeed points of 'unity', such as they were. Today this unity must surely appear more elusive. Methodological pluralism has increased enormously since 1977. As I argued in the last Chapter, anyone reading E. P. Sanders and Margaret Davies' *Studying the Synoptic Gospels*[8] will soon realise this. For the Old Testament (if one can even still use the term 'Old' Testament) Norman Gottwald's *The Hebrew Bible*[9] or John Barton's *Reading the Old Testament*[10] will have a similar effect.

What emerges from these recent works is that the introduction of methods from the social and literary sciences has forced Biblical scholars to be increasingly aware of an unavoidable and often bewildering range of methodological choices.[11] Not only must Biblical scholars make decisions about their own material. They must also decide about the merits or demerits of various social scientific and literary approaches as well. So if they read Gottwald's monumental *The Tribes of Israel*[12] they must decide not just about the material that he discusses but also about the Marxian analysis that he uses. Or if they read John Gager's *Kingdom and Community*[13] or Robert Carroll's *When Prophecy Failed*,[14] they must also decide about the merits or demerits of

[7] James D. G. Dunn, *Unity and Diversity in the New Testament*, SCM Press 1977. A second edition in 1990 updates the notes to take account of recent methodological developments, but not the text.

[8] E. P. Sanders and Margaret Davies, *Studying the Synoptic Gospels*, SCM Press 1989.

[9] Norman K. Gottwald, *The Hebrew Bible*, Fortress 1987.

[10] John Barton, *Reading the Old Testament*, Darton, Longman and Todd 1984.

[11] See further my *Theology and Sociology*, Chapman 1987 and Paulist 1988.

[12] Norman K. Gottwald, *The Tribes of Israel: A Sociology of the Religion of Liberated Israel*, 1250–1050, Orbis and SCM Press 1979.

[13] John G. Gager, *Kingdom and Community: the Social World of Early Christianity*, Prentice-Hall 1975.

[14] Robert P. Carroll, *When Prophecy Failed: Reactions and Responses to Failure in the Old Testament Prophetic Traditions*, SCM Press 1979.

cognitive dissonance theory in social-psychology.[15] Thus the methodological divisions already apparent amongst sociologists are now widely debated amongst Biblical scholars as well and in turn have had a powerful effect upon their work. And, since Gottwald has been heavily influenced by Liberation theologians, these methodological divisions and tensions can also be seen to be directly relevant to theology more widely.

(2) *No Agreed Definitions*

In view of these methodological tensions and conflicts within and across both disciplines, it is hardly surprising that agreed definitions are hard to find in either discipline. In theology it is notoriously difficult to reach any agreement about what actually constitutes 'theology'. Not only is there no agreed definition of the term (just as there is none in philosophy), but there are also wide variations in the range of subjects which are thought to be appropriate for a theology department to teach. In religious studies departments – with radical disagreement about the term 'religion', to which I shall return in Chapter 6 – these variations are if anything even wider. If once the perceived needs of the ordained ministry of specific churches largely dictated the constituent elements of theology departments, today this influence is considerably less.

Disagreement on precisely this issue was one of the less resolvable features of the Oxford Blackfriars Symposium that lasted for ten years and eventually produced *Sociology and Theology: Alliance and Conflict*.[16] It remains a unique collection, gathering together theologians and sociologists to debate some of the key methodological issues involved in relating the two disciplines. But it offers no hope of a unified definition of 'theology'. For the Dominican Timothy Radcliffe theology is 'the attempt to make sense of the gospel and the world in the mutually illuminating moment of their encounter'.[17] This experiential, non-academic understanding of theology stands in sharp contrast to my own definition of theology at the time: 'the

---

[15] See further my *Competing Convictions*, SCM Press 1989.

[16] David Martin, John Orme Mills and W. S. F. Pickering (edd.), *Sociology and Theology: Alliance and Conflict*, Harvester 1980.

[17] ibid., p. 157.

written and critical explication of the *sequelae* of individual religious beliefs and of the correlations and interactions between religious beliefs in general'.[18] David Martin, then professor of sociology at the London School of Economics, but also an Anglican priest, offered a more diffuse definition situated somewhere between these two understandings. For him theology 'articulates a "set" or frame which gathers together into one an approach to our personal and social being, a relation of temporal and eternal, a location of image or focus for harmony and perfection, a meaning which lies beyond our immediate apprehensions and which informs the world of natural and historic process'.[19] It was quite beyond even this Symposium of otherwise similarly disposed academics to produce a unified definition of theology which satisfied all three understandings!

In the 1960s sociology departments might have appeared to the outsider at least to be more unified. The severe cuts of the 1980s experienced in Britain at least and the declining popularity of the discipline everywhere have now radically changed this situation. Departments may now be very varied in the range of sub-disciplines that they offer, in the methods they adopt, and in what they consider to be key sociological areas. But even before this change of status there always were competing understandings of the nature of sociology as an academic discipline.

(3) *The Social Role of the Reading List*

If this is an accurate picture of the two disciplines, an obvious question arises. How do they in practice maintain a degree of coherence in the context of these tensions and conflicts? One obvious means of social control is through the reading list. Students coming to theology or sociology often have ideas about the disciplines and may already have done some reading. To establish coherence it becomes important to disabuse them of this reading as early as possible and to establish 'authentic' literature from the 'inauthentic'. Thus not all books about God are deemed by the professional theologian to be 'theology' and similarly not all books about society are deemed by the professional sociologist to be 'sociology'. The student must be

[18] See my *Theology and Social Structure*, Mowbrays 1977, p. 2f.
[19] Martin, Mills and Pickering, op. cit. p. 46.

initiated into authentic literature. Indeed, in the absence of agreed definitions about what constitutes theology or sociology (or philosophy, history, or English literature, if it comes to that) the reading list itself becomes a means of definition, or at least a means of circumscribing an area. Not surprisingly perhaps there are synchronic and diachronic variations (that is, variations within and across time) in reading lists – themselves eminently suitable for sociological study.

(4) The Social Status of Founding Fathers

The reading list naturally elevates some books at the expense of others. This in turn will be reflected in the stocking policy of local university bookshops and in the books that students generally buy and/or read. Common to most cognitive disciplines is a tendency especially to elevate the writings of a limited group of historical figures. Certain books from a previous age are regarded as seminal and it is incumbent upon students to read them carefully if they are to be 'properly' educated. In effect they become founding 'fathers' (founding 'mothers' are rare!).

The abiding status of Karl Marx amongst both sociologists and now theologians provides an obvious example of this process. Alistair Kee's recent *Marx and the Failure of Liberation Theology*[20] exemplifies this. He writes as a critic of Liberation theology from within and as one who has contributed very significantly to its study in Britain. In his Introduction he admits that his critique 'may come as a surprise to those who think of me as a defender of the theology of liberation. It is almost twenty years since I first came across the work of Gustavo Gutierrez Merino and since that time I have continually argued for the importance of liberation theology'.[21] In contrast, I suspect that many will be more surprised that the central plank of his critique is that Liberation theologians have not been sufficiently faithful to the writings of Marx.

Kee summarises this point – and it is significant that he talks, not wholly consistently, first of theologians 'ignoring' and then 'rejecting' Marx's criticisms – in the concluding paragraph of the book:

[20] Alistair Kee, *Marx and the Failure of Liberation Theology*, SCM Press and Trinity Press International 1990.
[21] ibid., p. ix.

'Liberation theologians have courageously led the way in ensuring that religion will no longer act as an opiate to the poor or an ideology in favour of the rich. In this they have accepted Marx's first and third criticisms of religion. But in steadfastly ignoring his second, ontological criticism, they have led the way into a cul de sac. Indeed they have not only ignored the ontological issue, they have deliberately rejected it. In this they have failed to comprehend the full implications of Marx's work.'[22]

However it is not just the writings of Marx, amongst Marxist sociologists and theologians, which function in this way – although the detailed textual, redactional and hermeneutical analyses of these writings are interesting and very closely resemble the work of traditional biblical scholarship. A work like Durkheim's *The Elementary Forms of the Religious Life* is treated in a very similar way – despite the now established evidence that most of the major (and very destructive) criticisms of it were made in the first decade of its appearance.[23] Both sociologists and theologians (and philosophers) show a remarkable propensity to work and rework well known criticisms of familiar works. They sometimes do this whilst being largely unaware of parallel discussions of the same works in other disciplines. Thus both sociologists and social anthropologists separately claim Durkheim, and both sociologists and theologians have separately used Troeltsch and H. R. Niebuhr.[24]

(5) *The Social Function of the Academic*
In this situation of methodological division, lack of agreed definitions, and socially relative reading-lists and founding fathers, the individual academic is given considerable power. It is usually the individual who determines the reading list and decides upon the balance of teaching to be allocated to the various founding fathers.

There is of course a difference between the largely modular system of teaching that characterises many American universities

[22] ibid., p. 282.
[23] See further W. S. F. Pickering, *Durkheim on Religion*, Routledge and Kegan Paul 1975, and *Durkheim's Sociology of Religion*, Routledge and Kegan Paul 1984.
[24] See further my *Competing Convictions*.

and the introductory courses taught by several academics that has until recently been more characteristic of British universities. Modular teaching often encourages the idiosyncrasies of gifted academics (controlled to an extent by student course question-naires), whereas introductory courses taught by several academics tend to suppress this. However, even in the British system of teaching, academics seldom hear each other actually teaching and often have external examiners covering areas well beyond their own specific expertise. As a result, in both contexts reading lists can be quite idiosyncratic and relatively unchallenged.

Further, the strong connection that has been held between teaching and personal research (now under considerable threat in Britain) may also foster the idiosyncratic. In this respect again there are similarities between theologians and sociologists. Amongst some individuals (perhaps including myself) with an interest in both disciplines, it can sometimes be quite difficult to know when they are functioning as theologians and when as sociologists.

(6) *Conceptual Similarities*

This point has wider implications for the discipline than is sometimes admitted. David Martin's work in Britain and Robert Bellah's work in the States provide very striking examples of the narrow dividing line that separates some forms of sociology from some forms of theology. Both are identifiable as straightforward, albeit imaginative, sociologists. Yet both over the last two decades have engaged in a number of theological debates. And in some of their writings, at least, it is difficult to decide whether they are functioning as sociologists or as theologians. It can even feel somewhat prosaic in their case to make such distinctions.

David Martin's writings are often characterised by a high literary style which in itself eludes tight boundaries between cognitive disciplines. In some of his writings there is also a strong polemical element, especially when he is defending traditional liturgical forms. Indeed, it is not difficult to see links between the two and to understand why he so despises what he regards as the mundane language of liturgical reformers. Both of these elements are present in what I believe to be one of his most original and creative books, *The Breaking of the Image*.[25] In the later sections of this book the boundaries between sociological analysis and theological polemic all but vanish. This is hardly surprising since he believes that modern liturgies are *both* socially dysfunctional and theologically 'unmusical'.

However it is in the less polemical early chapters of *The Breaking of the Image* that sociological and theological categories are most tantalisingly elided. Ostensibly he makes a clear distinction between the two disciplines. So he opens the book as follows:

> 'A sociologist has no remit to talk about God. If he were to talk directly about God he would immediately convert himself into a theologian or a philosopher of history or a prophet. To speak of God in the world is an act of unveiling. A prophet looks at the seeming flux of events and discerns the finger of God ... Sociologists are scientific scribes concerned with verifiable and fashionable statements and with more or less correct propositions about social processes ... They make connected sense out of the patterns that are thrown onto their field of social vision and hope that this connected sense is more controlled, more rich and rigorous than everyday observation ... But that has nothing to do with finding the finger of God, unless of course his finger is in the making of every social pie. If that is so they may safely ignore him. If God is up to everything then his activity may be elided.'[26]

On inspection the distinctions he makes here are far from clear-cut. Adjectives like 'fashionable' and 'rich' are paradoxically set alongside others like 'verifiable' and 'controlled'. Propositions about social processes are described as 'more or less correct'. And both theologians and sociologists would seem to be in the business of 'unveiling'.

As the book develops Martin unveils a series of tensions and paradoxes in religious language and action. Clearly influenced by semiotics, he identifies tensions between transcendence and unity, between the one and the many, between equality and fraternity, and between the cross as a symbol of suffering and the

[25] David Martin *The Breaking of the Image: A Sociology of Christian Theory and Practice*, Blackwell 1980.
[26] ibid., p. 1.

cross as an emblem of war. But having written about these tensions in a manner which could just as well come from the pen of a theologian, he argues with surely more than a hint of irony:

> 'In all this nothing has been said about God since reflection on social processes can know nothing whatever about God. Nevertheless God is meaningful to men through word and image and these images are the means of transcendence. Signs are the means of grace: God is known in the making of signs.'[27]

Robert Bellah writes with nothing approaching the literary style of David Martin. Nonetheless his books have just as often appealed to both sociological and theological audiences. In *Beyond Belief*[28] the links between his own religious beliefs and his work as a sociologist of religion become most apparent. Thus famously, after introducing the idea of 'symbolic realism' as a means of understanding religion, he argues:

> 'I believe that those of us who study religion must have a kind of double vision; at the same time that we try to study religious systems as objects we need also to apprehend them as ourselves religious subjects. Neither evolutionist nor historical relativist nor theological triumphalist positions should allow us to deny that religion is one. I don't mean to say that all religions are saying the same thing in doctrinal or ethical terms; obviously they are not. But religion is one for the same reason that science is one – because man is one. No expression of man's attempt to grasp the meaning and unity of his existence, not even a myth of a primitive Australian, is without meaning and value to me . . . If this seems to confuse the role of theologian and scientist, of teaching religion and teaching about religion, then so be it. The radical split between knowledge and commitment that exists in our culture and in our universities is not ultimately tenable. Differentiation has gone about as far as it can go. It is time for a new integration.'[29]

Six years later he was writing in *The New Religious Consciousness* that 'the values, attitudes, and beliefs of the oriental religious groups, the human-potential movement, and even a group like the Christian World Liberation Front, as well as the more

[27] ibid., p. 16.
[28] Robert N. Bellah, *Beyond Belief*, Harper and Row 1970.
[29] ibid., p. 257.

flexible of the radical political groups, would be consonant with the new regime and its needs . . . the new age groups would be, under such an option, the vanguard of a new age'.[30] And in the following decade he was, as has already been noted in the previous chapter, a key figure in producing *Habits of the Heart*[31] with all its hopes that communities, and especially religious communities, would be instrumental in embedding values into society. For Bellah and for the other contributors to *Habits of the Heart* the notion of 'community' is defined in terms which owe something to the social sciences but much also to moral philosophy. Thus, in the definition cited earlier, a 'community' is for them:

> 'a group of people who are socially interdependent, who participate together in discussion and decision making, and who share certain practices that both define the community and are nurtured by it. Such a community is not quickly formed. It almost always has a history and so is also a community of memory, defined in part by its past and its memory of its past.'[32]

By adding the last two sentences the authors exclude such groups as deviant gangs or Hitler's Youth Movement. But this is an exclusion which would traditionally make more sense morally than sociologically. I will return to this broad issue in Chapter 6. Here it is sufficient to note that, however confusing they might be, these elisions do exist within sociology. If they confuse, they surely confuse at a distinctly higher level than the elisions made by the theologically or sociologically naive. Bellah and Martin may be confusing – albeit very differently confusing – but they are manifestly not themselves naively confused. Rather they act as a warning to all those who imagine that theology and sociology are in every approach methodologically distinct.

In Martin's case it is semiotics that provides a link between his sociology and his theology. In Bellah's case it is his notion of

---

[30] Charles Y. Glock and Robert N. Bellah (edd.), *The New Religious Consciousness*, University of California Press 1976, p. 352.

[31] Robert N. Bellah, Richard Madsen, William M. Sullivan, Ann Swidler and Steven M. Tipton, *Habits of the Heart: Middle America Observed*, Hutchinson 1985, and *Individualism and Commitment in American Life: Readings on the Theme of Habits of the Heart*, Harper and Row 1987.

[32] *Habits of the Heart*, p. 335.

symbolic realism and his constant stress upon values and implicit theology (evident also in his notion of civil religion).[33] Sometimes it is simply attention to social context or *Sitz im Leben* (to use a more theological term) which provides a link. Again, both hermeneutics and phenomenology have had profound and parallel influences on both disciplines. It can be quite difficult today to distinguish a theologian influenced by structuralist literary criticism from a structuralist literary critic who is interested in the Bible. Amongst liberation theologians – and amongst applied theologians more generally – it is the concept of *praxis* from the Frankfurt School that provides the link. An increasing tendency amongst theology post-graduates to do empirical research is also forcing them to learn quantitative skills thought once to be the preserve of social scientists. And sociologists of religion seem to be increasingly aware that the theological nuances of a religious group should form at least a part of their sociological understanding.

(7) *Sociological Uses of Theology*

Another point of convergence has seen a number of sociologists of religion using theology as a means of increasing their *sociological* understanding of religion. Weber's cognitive approach to the sociology of religion always did mean that theological ideas ought to be explored at times if religious phenomena are to be properly understood. However, recently there have been a number of successful collaborations between sociologists and theologians exploring religious phenomena as social realities.

One of the most striking examples of this is the recent collection by Donald Capps and James E. Dittes, *The Hunger of the Heart: Reflections on the Confessions of Augustine*.[34] Most unusually, this has been produced as a monograph for the Society for the Scientific Study of Religion. It is unusual for several reasons. It contains no statistical data; its central concern is with one of the classics of theology, namely Augustine's *Confessions*; its two editors are both pastoral theologians, albeit

---

[33] See Robert N. Bellah, *The Broken Covenant: American Civil Religion in Time of Trial*, Seabury 1975.

[34] Society for the Scientific Study of Religion, Monograph Series, No. 8, Purdue University 1990.

with obvious social scientific knowledge; and the methods it uses are eclectic but predominantly drawn from psychoanalytic traditions. Yet having said that, it is justified by its editors as a contribution more to the social sciences than to theology.

The editors draw together twenty studies of the *Confessions*, many of which have appeared in the *Journal for the Scientific Study of Religion* over the last two decades, placing them in subject groups together with summaries and connecting critical commentary. The latter is always coherent and empirically illuminating. Their general introduction also ably defends the collection as an exercise in the social sciences (albeit drawing upon several disciplines including critical theology) and points to some of its lacunae. And it is the theologian Donald Capps who produces one of the most thoughtful contributions, distinguishing between 'guilt' and 'shame' in the *Confessions* and arguing that it was the latter which most shaped Augustine's early theological stances.

The collection is divided into six parts which consider in sequence the propositions that Augustine in the *Confessions* was the product of child abuse or maladjustment, that he had strong oedipal tendencies, that he was profoundly narcissistic, and that the *Confessions* itself proved (or not) to be therapeutic psychologically and/or spiritually for Augustine. It also reprints the classical scholar E. R. Dodds' famous article from the 1920s 'Augustine's *Confessions*: A Study of Spiritual Maladjustment' and the psychoanalyst Charles Kligerman's seminal 'A Psychoanalytic Study of the *Confessions* of St. Augustine' of the 1950s. In various ways all of the other articles respond to the empirical approaches to the text that they pioneered.

One of the strong features of this collection is the way that it brings out the conflicts amongst scholars generated by using the social sciences in this way to study a classic work of theology. Because the *Confessions* itself contains so many intriguing hints about Augustine as a person and especially about his relationship to his mother, even those who are less than persuaded by psychoanalytic terminology will still gain much from this collection.

The Hunger of the Heart, at times unwittingly, suggests a new genre of scholarship. The *Confessions* has been a major influence on subsequent accounts of conversion experience, and the collection is aware of, but seldom develops, the hermeneutical insight that the work itself, whatever Augustine intended, has become an independent social variable. Further, sociologists might have expected some discussion of notions such as that of liminality, since this is patently a liminal work by a major, but highly troubled, thinker at a key point of social and personal change. Once sociologists of religion adopt the approach pioneered here they may soon discover many fascinating new caves to explore. Sociological readings of theology are still in their infancy.

(8) *Theological Critiques of Sociology*

So are theological critiques of sociology. One of the more startling innovations of the 1980s has been the appearance of theologically inspired critiques of sociology. These have usually taken the form (as in my own writings) of critiques of particular sociological concepts, such as secularisation. Here it is argued that a theologically nuanced approach to religious phenomena can act as an important corrective to some of the cruder forms of positivism. So for example, I have for long argued that the role of theology should be taken into account in sociological explanations of ecumenism.[35] It is *sociologically* inadequate to explain the modern ecumenical movement simply in terms of secularisation or organisational theory.

However a few scholars have offered wholesale theological critiques of sociology. Amongst these David Lyon's *Sociology and the Human Image* and John Milbank's *Theology and Social Theory: Beyond Secular Reason* are the most startling. They write from very different theological perspectives – Lyon is an evangelical and Milbank an Anglo-Catholic – but both are convinced that theology offers a fundamental challenge to sociology. Each devotes a major part of his book to showing that sociology is not a value-free enterprise and that particular sociologists have implicit, but often unacknowledged, ideological commitments that shape their perspectives. In this task they are both highly successful.

[35] See my article 'British Theology as a Sociological variable', in Michael Hill (ed), *A Sociological Yearbook of Religion in Britain 7*, SCM Press 1974.

Where they are less successful is in their (divergent) suggestions of some alternative 'Christian sociology'. For Lyon it is a biblically derived anthropology which has 'the unique potential to cut through some of the contradictions (of sociology), provide direction and aid decision, not from a purely human-centered perspective but from a God-centered one'.[36] Thus, for him:

> 'A Christian perspective in sociology is founded upon a biblical understanding of human sociality. The key assumption is that, because our Maker has told us about himself and ourselves, disclosing his mind to us through a book, that here is the basis for a truly human outlook on the world.'[37]

I suspect that Milbank would label this an erroneous 'foundationalism'. For him, 'Christian sociology is distinctive simply because it explicates, and adopts the vantage point of, a distinct society, the Church'.[38] Thus, as befits their differing theological commitments, Lyon's 'Christian sociology' is biblically based, whereas that of Milbank is ecclesially based. Yet both authors offer their alternatives only in outline and at the very end of their analyses of sociology. Given this, it would perhaps be premature to judge their alternatives too harshly.

However one feature of their work does deserve critical comment. Despite many illuminating observations about the values that underlie the work of particular sociologists, both have a tendency to dismiss 'secular' sociology *tout court* even whilst themselves adopting forms of analysis clearly derived from this sociology. Milbank provides the most striking examples of this tendency. For instance, he argues:

> 'For sociology, religion is a component of the protected "human" sphere, although this sphere is sometimes (for Durkheim) made to coincide with the schematic possibility of theoretic understanding. But although religion is recognised and protected, it is also "policed", or kept rigorously behind the bounds of the possibility of empirical understanding. Hence sociology is inevitably at variance with the perspectives

[36] David Lyon, *Sociology and the Human Image*, IVP 1983, p. 190.
[37] ibid., p. 193.
[38] John Milbank, *Theology and Social Theory: Beyond Secular Reason*, Blackwell 1990, p. 381.

of many traditional religions, which make no separation between "religious" and "empirical" reality, and who do not distinguish their sense of value from the stratified arrangements of times, persons, and places in their own society. Sociology's "policing of the sublime" exactly coincides with the actual operations of secular society which excludes religion from its modes of "discipline and control", while protecting it as a "private" value, and sometimes invoking it at the public level to overcome the antimony of a purely instrumental and goalless rationality, which is yet made to bear the burden of ultimate political purpose ... I am going to show how all twentieth-century sociology of religion can be exposed as a secular policing of the sublime. Deconstructed in this fashion, the entire subject evaporates into the pure ether of the secular will-to-power.'[39]

Significantly, although he does apply this critique of sociology of religion to Berger and to Bellah, he makes no use whatsoever of David Martin. Had he attempted to do so, his hyperbole would surely have become apparent. Martin has, after all, spent most of his career as a sociologist of religion criticising the very tendencies now attacked by Milbank. Furthermore, despite the serious and important points that are made in Milbank's critique, it manifestly depends upon the very sociological procedures that he is criticising. He is, for example, asserting that there is a socio-structural link between assumptions of sociologists and power relationships within society. This is a shrewd observation, but it is a *sociological* observation, and it is (*mutatis mutandis*) the sort of observation that sociologists of religion have been making effectively about some churches ever since Marx. To dismiss the latter *tout court*, whilst still maintaining the former, seems scarcely consistent.

All of this a far cry from the Berger Appendix with which I began. In some respects the circle is now complete. Berger began his career as a sociologist in a theological seminary, but then moved into a sociology department whilst continuing to write about theology and theologians albeit from the high-ground of sociology. Today a somewhat humbled sociology has been

[39] ibid., pp. 105–6.

accepted with increasing enthusiasm by theologians and by theology departments. As mentioned earlier, in Britain it is now quite usual for the latter to have a resident sociologist and it is *de rigeur* for biblical scholars to have at least some acquaintance with the social sciences. And my own path of graduating in both disciplines is no longer the functional equivalent of a literary *hapax logomenon*. In short Berger's warnings now appear quaint.

To express all this, perhaps too epigramatically, just as theologians and even Christian ethicists are becoming more detached and empirical, so sociologists seem to be becoming more engaged and inter-subjective.

Part 2

The Environment

3

Faith in the Countryside

Within the secular world there has recently been a renewed ethical interest in ecological issues. Sometimes this has taken the form of a concern about global ecology – overpopulation in the world, industrial pollution, destruction of rain forests, concern about the ozone layer, the use of non-renewable fossil fuels, biotechnology, genetic release, nuclear pollution, nuclear holocaust, etc. The list is long and grows ever longer. At other times ethical interest in ecological issues takes a more local form. Britain still enjoys a rich and varied countryside, yet it is a countryside subject to continuous change from the pressures of a mobile and predominantly suburban population.

In this chapter I will focus upon the more local form of this ecological concern. In the next two chapters I will turn to the broader issues. The latter are clearly important, but all too often they appear depressingly impervious to moral change. Charles Elliott expresses this with blunt clarity:

> 'Our guilt, then, is total. There is no way out of it. I may protest about the arms race, simplify my life style, eat lentils not meat, opt out of the consumer society, work in a co-operative, constantly examine my presuppositions and ethical assumptions. That may be good and worthy, but in the end I am caught. I am caught because I am human; and I am human in this society at this time.'[1]

Elliott's sentiments are morally depressing precisely because he is himself, in addition to being a theologian, an expert on development economics. If anyone ought to be capable of

[1] Charles Elliott, *Praying the Kingdom: Towards a Political Spirituality*, DLT 1985, p. 5.

45

devising effective economic strategies to change the world, it is
he. Yet he argues, in the context of the international trade in raw
materials which so deeply affects the Third World, that:

> 'The most powerful single mechanism for removing well-being
> from one group and bestowing it on another seems to be
> beyond the control of *any single group*. Producers do not
> control prices. Consumers don't. Despite much populist
> comment, in most cases multi-national corporations don't.
> Each may have some influence, and that influence may be
> unequal. There is, however, no single authority; no equivalent
> to a planning committee which makes an unambiguous
> decision; no identifiable "them" to whom one can talk or
> against whom one can rail.'[2]

Naivety and tokenism are so widespread in much of the
current concern about global ecology. In contrast, Elliott acts as
an important, even if uncomfortable, iconoclast. I will return to
his specifically theological contribution to these issues in
Chapter 7. For the moment it is sufficient to note his deep
reservations. Global issues seem to be particularly resilient to
moral challenges.

But perhaps localised ecological issues are more responsive to
moral action. The fact that global issues appear so impervious
and morally depressing, certainly should not exonerate us from a
concern about our own countryside. In this situation, the report
of the Archbishop's Commission on Rural Areas, *Faith in the
Countryside*,[3] has been awaited with considerable interest. Here
is a clear example of the Church of England responding to the
wider ecological concerns apparent in the secular world, and yet
still making specific recommendations to the Nation and to the
Churches on how they should act in the future.

I

In this chapter I will review this report in the context of these
wider concerns. In the process I hope to uncover some of the
theological and ethical criteria that might better inform the

[2] ibid., pp. 6–7.
[3] Archbishop of Canterbury's Commission on Rural Areas, *Faith in the
Countryside*, Church House Publishing 1990.

debate and offer a critique of the structural challenges that the report makes to the Churches.

In the long-established practice of Anglican reports, *Faith in the Countryside* is guided at the outset by an empirical analysis of the secular world. On the first page it states:

> 'In recent years there has been a remarkable change in the make-up of the rural population. This has brought to villages a growing number of incomers with higher proportions of the elderly and the more affluent among them. The overall picture leaves no doubt about the tensions between those who traditionally regarded the countryside as their own and their work place, and the new arrivals. Interest in the countryside is by no means the preserve of those who live and work there; urban dwellers too have claims on and aspirations for the countryside they wish to enjoy. The integration of new villagers is a challenge for voluntary organisations and particularly for the Church, among whose tasks is the reconciling of differences in the local community.'[4]

Inevitably *Faith in the Countryside* invites comparison with the parallel report of the Archbishop of Canterbury's Commission on Urban Priority Areas, *Faith in the City*.[5] The latter has, as I affirmed earlier, been a very significant moral achievement and has forced both Churches and Government to take more seriously the plight of urban priority areas. It has made possible the Church Urban Fund and inspired a new generation of Christians and others to engage in a variety of imaginative inner-city projects. A disproportionately rural Church of England has been forced to take urban outreach more seriously.

But, of course, serious problems have remained in rural areas. From the side of the Churches the problems are numerous. Stories of single-handed clergy looking after twelve, and possibly even fifteen, parishes have become common currency. Free Church collapse, apparent in many urban priority areas, has also characterised many rural areas. Even high church-going rates, once thought to be the preserve of the countryside, have collapsed. In North Northumberland today general church-

---

[4] ibid., p. v.
[5] Archbishop of Canterbury's Commission on Urban Priority Areas, *Faith in the City*, Church House Publishing 1985.

going rates (9%) can be matched by those in Morpeth and Tynemouth,[6] and are significantly less than those in the City of York (11%). And parts of rural Wales, which as recently as 1950 recorded general church-going rates of 66%, today record just 17%.[7] Only seasonal conformity remains high in the countryside.

From the side of the rural community at large, problems are just as serious. There are increasing difficulties for the poor and the elderly in rural areas suffering from cut-backs in council-housing, public transport, village schools and local health services, and in the gradual demise of village shops. Affluent urban dwellers coming to live in the countryside bring some wealth to rural areas but perhaps even more problems. Their wealth distorts the cost of local housing. They make comparatively little use of rural transport, schools or shops. And, in any case, their rural homes may in reality be infrequently used 'second homes'. All of this brings with it problems for indigenous rural populations, in Britain as well as elsewhere in the affluent North.

From an ethical perspective, it is important to stress at the outset that in terms of populations these are not equal problems. England is at least 80% urban in terms of its population. In relation to this, clergy in the Church of England, and church and chapel buildings in a number of other denominations, are still disproportionately rural.[8] Yet, despite growth in rural populations in some parts of the country over the last two decades, England remains an urban nation, and has been so since 1851.

It is in this context that any comparison between *Faith in the City* and *Faith in the Countryside* should be made. Does the ACORA report complement the ACUPA report, presenting a rounded vision for the future, or does it detract from it and return the Churches to confusion? I will seek to address this question under three broad headings – which themselves correspond to the three sections of the report itself – theology, the Nation, and the Churches.

[6] See my *Competing Convictions*, SCM Press 1989.
[7] See my *The Myth of the Empty Church*, SPCK 1992.
[8] See my *Beyond Decline*, SCM Press 1988.

2

Faith in the City was most heavily criticised within the Churches for its theology. Nigel Biggar at Oxford and Duncan Forrester at Edinburgh each produced extended theological critiques of the report. They judged that theology came too late in the report, that it was too elliptical, and that it had not permeated the rest of the report.

The authors of *Faith in the Countryside* were doubtless aware of these criticisms and have responded well to the first two. The theological chapter is placed first in the new report and, under the guidance of Brian Horne of King's College London, it is a model of clarity. It argues successfully that a doctrine of creation does have direct relevance to a Green Age and that the biblical concept of 'a person' as being 'a person in community' offers a direct challenge to the dominant individualism that our society has inherited from the Enlightenment, and which I criticised through MacIntyre in Chapter 1.

One slight surprise for non-Anglicans reading this theological chapter might be that so few Anglican theologians are cited in what is after all an Anglican report. Anglicans can be proud of a distinguished line of theologians who have written on the theme of creation – from Archbishop William Temple to John Polkinghorne[9] and Keith Ward[10] today. Yet they are mostly conspicuous by their absence in this otherwise important chapter.

However, it is in relation to the third criticism that *Faith in the Countryside* is as vulnerable as its predecessor. *Faith in the City* was most stridently criticised on theological grounds because its central moral concepts were apparently moulded more by secular culture than by Christian theology. Nigel Biggar expressed this criticism as follows:

> 'Our examination of the principal ethical concepts employed in *Faith in the City* – compassion, justice, community and the fulfilment of individual potential – has revealed a consistent failure to use them in a theologically critical manner. Similar

[9] John Polkinghorne, *One World*, SPCK 1986, *Science and Creation: The Search for Understanding*, SPCK 1988, and *Science and Providence*, SPCK 1989.
[10] Keith Ward, *The Divine Image: the Foundations of Christian Morality*, SPCK 1976 and *Rational Theology and the Creativity of God*, Blackwell 1982.

complaints have been made about the report's use of economic and sociological concepts. We have attributed this failure to the premise that the theological framework in which these moral concepts stand makes no significant claim upon their substance; and we have argued that this premise is false.'[11]

From the analysis contained in Chapter 2 it will be apparent that I do not wholly share Biggar's confidence that theological and sociological methods can any longer be distinguished so neatly. Nevertheless, his central contention is important. Once Christian ethics loses all of its theological distinctiveness, it loses everything. 'Christian ethics in secular worlds' simply becomes 'ethics in secular worlds'. That would (*pace* Biggar) be far too harsh a judgement on *Faith in the City*, but nevertheless it has sufficient resonance to make many theologians uneasy.

And sadly it is an uneasiness which may also find resonances in the theological method adopted in *Faith in the Countryside*. Here too, theology is barely mentioned in the next four chapters of the report (concerned with the Nation). It surfaces properly only when the report considers the Churches. It is, perhaps, archetypically Anglican to do theology and to pass political judgements, but not to make the link between the two explicit. It is precisely this which so infuriates moral theologians from Reformed and Roman Catholic traditions.

Duncan Forrester well illustrates this Reformed Church infuriation. Despite considerable sympathy with the overall political bias of *Faith in the City* (probably more sympathy than Nigel Biggar), he is equally dismissive of the lack of theological direction in the report. In a very early response to the report, he began his argument as follows:

'There appear to be two distinct theologies in *Faith in the City*, which sit rather uneasily together and do not seem to be closely related. There is an *implicit* theology which rarely appears on the surface of the argument but is undoubtedly influential in the shaping of the method and approach of the Report; for this I have considerable enthusiasm. And there is an *explicit* theology, laid out in chapters three and four, which it must be said is bland in a distinctively Anglican way, and

---

[11] Nigel Biggar, *Theological Politics: A Critique of 'Faith in the City'*, Latimer House Publication, Oxford 1988, p. 43.

academic in the sense of being detached. It is not surprising that this theology is not integrated in a wholly convincing way with the rest of the Report as it is hardly capable of throwing light on the great issues which are addressed.'[12]

A more considered verdict that he gave later was distinctly more complimentary about the report itself. He now acknowledged that it 'will certainly appear in the history books as a milestone in the church's contribution to public affairs. In a way the Commission did speak with the world's voice'.[13] Yet he still maintained that theology had failed adequately to permeate the report:

'There *is* theology in *Faith in the City*; the best part of two chapters of it. But although some other sections of the report sound prophetic, and clearly share in the anger, frustration, and hopes of people in the UPAs, although most of the language is clear and direct, in the theological sections the language becomes tentative, detached, and almost apologetic – "It may be argued . . .", "It may be felt . . .", "We may well be asked . . .", "If the policies of any government can be shown to be making the plight of some classes of citizens actually worse . . . it is a clear duty for the Church to sound a warning that our society may be losing the 'compassionate' character that is still desired by the majority of its members". There are lots of nods in the direction of tolerance, consensus, community, and co-operation, but also a refusal to look conflicts of interest and social unrest in the face. These, we are told, are "grey areas" with which theology finds great difficulty in engaging: "We have little tradition of initiating conflict and coping with it creatively. We are not at home in the tough secular milieu of social and political activism." That honest and revealing remark points to the fundamental problem of modern British theology in this connection: its home is the senior common room or the seminary. It accordingly has peculiar difficulty in entering into productive dialogue with the influential social theories of today, whether associated with the New Right or with Marxism.'[14]

[12] Duncan B. Forrester, 'The Theology of the Report' in *Faith in the Scottish City*, Occasional Paper 8, Centre for Theology and Public Issues, Edinburgh University 1986, p. 11.

[13] Duncan B. Forrester, *Beliefs, Values and Policies: Conviction Politics in a Secular Age*, Clarendon 1989, p. 84.

[14] ibid., p. 85.

I have quoted this at length because it pin-points a tension that runs through many attempts to do Christian ethics in secular worlds. Unfortunately Forrester seems in danger at times of confusing tactics with substance. And what for him are clear signs of weak faith, or even Anglican 'blandness', may in reality be stylistic conventions intended simply to express theological humility. For tactical reasons it surely might sometimes be less appropriate than at other times to engage in the finer points of theological debate. Exponents of Christian ethics who engage in sustained ethical dialogue with interested parties in science, medicine or business studies – unless these parties are themselves explicitly religious – typically do tend to talk more about 'values' than about explicit theological commitments. And perhaps they should do.

But this is a matter of tactics or style. Explicit theological notions can easily become weapons, rather than sources of dialogue, if they are offered as bold challenges to otherwise secular groups. In the process, dialogue would soon become one-sided and extremely short-lived. Why should otherwise secular professionals find theological notions ethically informative when they do not share the vision and the context in worship that sustains these notions?

It is for this very reason that theology is more prominent in some of the chapters that follow than in others. So explicit theology is offered only tentatively at the end of Chapter 5 on biotechnology (as it was in Ramsey's original book) because it was concerned, when originally delivered, with entering into a dialogue with scientists who may or may not themselves be religiously committed. And the final chapter on AIDS and Social Policy contains no explicit theology at all. This is not because theology is unimportant or uninformative on the topic, but because the context in which it was fashioned was not itself a religiously committed one.

This *is* tactics or style. It is not about substance. The actual values that are used in the AIDS and Social Policy chapter are derived (albeit implicitly) from Christian resources. They are not simply values snatched from the air or distilled from 'common sense'. Yet they are still values which are capable, I believe, of being used in quite secular worlds and which might be heard sympathetically outside overtly Christian contexts. Just as Churches can be harbingers of Christian values that they neither wholly exemplify nor fully understand, as I argued earlier, so society more broadly may still be influenced by values whose theological justification is appreciated by very few within it. I will return to this broad issue in Chapters 6 and 7. For the moment it is important to distinguish between the values themselves (which may still influence society) and the theological justification of these values (which may be largely incomprehensible to a society that no longer worships).

Something like this may have been the general assumption that underlay *Faith in the City*. However, it was not the defence offered later by Anthony Harvey. As the architect of the chapter that Biggar and Forrester so vehemently attacked, he was clearly stung by the criticism that the theology in the report 'had been widely criticised as "weak", "inadequate" and "incoherent"'.[15] In response he argued that the authors of *Faith in the City* had 'believed that their primary task was theological'.[16] Yet they had also believed that a 'systematic' approach to theology would have been inappropriate given their subject-matter. They were, instead, trying to develop a more local and more contextualised approach to theology than would have been possible had they adopted some 'scheme' or 'system'.

As so often in theological debates, much of this discussion has been at cross-purposes. Some of the criticisms directed at the theology of *Faith in the City* might have implied that it lacked 'system'. Most were much more concerned that its explicit theology was either too obtuse or had failed to inform the underlying values in the rest of the report. For Forrester much of the problem was simply that the theological sections 'gave the impression of being inserted somewhat artificially, rather than informing the whole analysis of the report'.[17] Harvey apparently missed that point. But then perhaps Forrester confused tactics and style with a lack of faith and substance.

[15] Anthony Harvey, 'Introduction: An Alternative Theology?', in Harvey (ed.), *Theology in the City: A Theological Response to 'Faith in the City'*, SPCK 1989, p. 1.
[16] ibid.
[17] Forrester, 1989, op. cit. p. 84.

Personally I appreciated the theological sections of *Faith in the City* rather more than Biggar or Forrester. I believe that they do make some good and sustained points. *Faith in the Countryside* does this perhaps slightly better. Yet neither continues to use these resources explicitly when discussing political issues. And for an explicitly denominational report in an ecumenical age (even one written for the Nation), that was surely a *tactical* error. It could scarcely fail to give the impression to other Christian traditions that almost everything that appears in the chapters addressed to the Nation might equally have been written by a purely secular political lobby group.

3

With the help of experts such as Howard Newby, perhaps the leading rural sociologist in Britain today, the analysis and recommendations in the report for the Nation at large can certainly stand favourable comparison with *Faith in the City*.

The countryside is currently undergoing crucial technological and demographic changes. Agriculture directly employs only one-in-seven rural workers today. As in urban areas, service industries are becoming increasingly important. Retired people from urban areas are increasingly coming to live in the countryside – together with some urban dwellers with second homes – bringing some affluence but also changes. As mentioned earlier, house prices have soared and have become ever less accessible to the rural poor. A decline in council housing and in inexpensive rented accommodation has caused real hardship. Affluent newcomers do not require local public transport and do their main shopping in urban supermarkets not in village stores. And an increasingly elderly population has caused problems for rural schools. Even tourism in the countryside has brought new demands.

Faith in the Countryside responds vigorously to all of these changes. The authors would like to see new common land and increased public access to the countryside. They would like to see a Government review of rural transport and health facilities and provision for training and retraining of the rural workforce. They would like to see a balance between strengthening the rural economy and protecting and sustaining the countryside. They would like the Government to lift restrictions which forbid local authorities to use much of the finance gained from council house sales to provide new affordable low-cost rural housing. And they are conscious that Churches and local voluntary groups can also assist in many of these areas.

However, if the authors had made theology more explicit in this section of the report, they might have noticed a rather glaring omission from all of this. Amongst Christian ethicists concerned with rural issues, there has recently been considerable discussion about the morality of intensive animal farming. Andrew Linzey[18] at Essex and Stephen Clark[19] at Liverpool (both Anglicans as it happens) have been prominent in this debate. Yet the issue is barely mentioned in *Faith in the Countryside*. This omission is really very surprising. Of course, in the context it would have been a very contentious issue and doubtless it would have risked alienating some rural dwellers. Yet it is difficult to see how a report that is committed to contextualised theology and to localised ecology could simply by-pass the issue.

In its political recommendations *Faith in the Countryside* seems to be following the path set by *Faith in the City*. David Donnison, who was for five years Chairman of the Supplementary Benefits Commission and is now Professor of Town Planning at Glasgow, argued that *Faith in the City*, together with reports from a number of voluntary agencies, filled an important gap once occupied by (largely abolished) Government Commissions.[20] *Faith in the Countryside*, especially with Lord Prior at its helm, will no doubt be seen in a similar light. Whilst seeing the importance of this, it does have an obvious danger. Political considerations rather than theological vision can soon control its recommendations to the Nation. Perhaps neither the Government nor the countryside lobby will be too displeased this time

[18] Andrew Linzey, *Christianity and the Rights of Animals*, SPCK 1987, and *Compassion for Animals*, SPCK 1988: see also Linzey and Tom Regan (edd.) *Animals and Christianity: A Book of Readings*, SPCK 1988.

[19] Stephen R. L. Clark, *The Moral Status of Animals*, OUP 1977, and *The Nature of the Beast: Are Animals Moral?*, OUP 1982.

[20] cf. David Donnison, 'The Significance of the Report', in *Faith in the Scottish City*, op. cit., and Forrester, 1989, op. cit., p. 84.

around. This at least will not be dubbed by unattributable political sources as 'a Marxist report'. Yet other Christians may suspect that this is because it lacks sustained theological, rather than political, teeth.

4

Theology does return to the final part of *Faith in the Countryside*, but here it is the analysis which is sadly flawed. The intentions of its authors are honourable. They genuinely desire to see an invigorated rural Church. They wish to encourage collaborative forms of ministry, no longer dependent on freehold, and much greater ecumenical co-operation. They wish rural Churches to be more heavily involved in such issues as housing and local transport. And they clearly received expert advice from scholars such as, Leslie Francis[21] and Anthony Russell[22] (a member of ACORA). Yet their conclusions are confused and partial.

In the late nineteenth century the Church of England and the Free Churches built vigorously against a declining rural population.[23] In fact, in those areas of Britain which have been studied most closely, the second half of the nineteenth century was the busiest time of rural church building and restoration for three hundred years. It was also the time when the countryside came nearest to having a resident incumbent in every parish. Yet 1851 marks the moment at which England ceased to be a rural society. Rural and urban populations grew rapidly in the first half of the nineteenth century, but just urban areas in the second half. London and many other urban areas doubled or trebled in population, whilst rural areas depopulated.

The result of all of this, as I tried to show in *Competing Convictions*, was that by 1901 whole areas of the countryside – Northumberland, Lincolnshire, North Yorkshire, Norfolk,

[21] Leslie J. Francis, *Rural Anglicanism*, Collins 1985, and *Partnership in Rural Education*, Collins 1986.

[22] Anthony Russell, *The Clerical Profession*, SPCK 1980, and *The Country Parish*, SPCK 1986.

[23] For the argument that follows, see my *Competing Convictions* and *The Myth of the Empty Church*, op. cit.

Suffolk, Devon, Cornwall and many pockets of countryside elsewhere – had more seats in their churches and chapels than they had people. In parts of rural Wales, churches and chapels were left with two, and sometimes three, times as many seats as resident population. The Church of England, despite strenuous efforts in urban areas, found itself stranded. By 1901 58% of its parishes were catering for populations of less than 1,000 people.[24] In a now urban society the Church of England remained a rural Church.

This was one of the key problems that the *Paul Report*[25] addressed in 1964. Leslie Paul found that 42% of Anglican incumbents still had parishes of less than 1,500 people. Altogether they were ministering to just 11% of the population of England. And this is the problem which the Sheffield formula[26] has attempted to address since 1974 – albeit by redressing balances between Anglican dioceses, not by ensuring balances within them. My own empirical research suggests that it still remains a problem today.

However, in *Faith in the Countryside* this problem is simply ignored. What the authors observe instead is a rural population that has grown somewhat over the last two decades and rural churches that are now struggling to survive with a decreasing number of clergy. Further, since it is in the countryside that Free Churches have collapsed, they argue that it has become important for Anglicans to provide more rural clergy. So they conclude:

> 'This will mean an adjustment to the Sheffield formula in the short term with clergy losses coming from the urban and suburban areas.' (8–50).

Unfortunately this conclusion effectively undermines the strategy inherent in *Faith in the City* and commits the Church of England to remaining too rural a Church in an urban society. It is also a profoundly muddled conclusion – economically, strategically and theologically.

[24] Calculated from *Population Census* 1901.
[25] Leslie Paul, *The Deployment and Payment of the Clergy*, Church Information Office 1964.
[26] For a description of the Sheffield Formula, see *Faith in the City* and the Church Commissioners, *The Historic Resources of the Church of England*, 1986.

It is muddled economically – not least because its relation to other conclusions is uncosted. Several of the other conclusions in the report would commit the Church to a considerable increase in expenditure on clerical incomes and expenses, and to a decrease in revenue from the Church Commissioners. Stipends are to be raised and perhaps graduated, expenses are also to be raised and computers provided for all, and wives are to receive a remuneration of some £2,000. At the same time, former vicarages, rectories and church schools need no longer be sold to the highest bidder. The needs of the local community – whether for recreation or inexpensive housing – must be considered first. And the Church Commissioners should be restricted to ecologically sound investments. Added together these various uncosted commitments will certainly be expensive. For example, there is clear American evidence[27] that ethical investment policies (despite their claims to the contrary) considerably reduce revenues. Important though these commitments are, if implemented they can only mean that an increase in stipendiary rural clergy will divert a very sizeable proportion of the Church of England's remaining funds to the countryside.

It is muddled strategically. The authors seem to realise that this is a short-term policy and that the future will depend upon non-stipendiary forms of ministry (ordained or lay) and greater ecumenical collaboration. But the way to encourage the latter is not by increasing rural subsidy. If the countryside is to become more self-sufficient, then increased subsidy will not help local churches to achieve this. Stipends since the *Paul Report* have been made more equal and comparative clerical poverty considerably relieved. But the result of this, together with the considerable inflation of the 1970s, has been that few country parishes in the Church of England now raise even a third of the £19,000 per annum that the report acknowledges that it costs to have a stipendiary incumbent. Whilst such a level of subsidy continues, alternative forms of rural ministry will naturally remain slow to develop.

It is muddled theologically. The authors reach no decision

[27] See Sam Mueller in *Sociological Analysis*, 1991.

about the long-term alternatives to stipendiary ministry. Reviewing the possibilities, they observe:

> 'The evidence of the Rural Church Project indicates that many parishioners would prefer a full-time stipendiary minister looking after a cluster of parishes, even if that minister lived at some distance, to a part-time minister living in the parish.' (8–75)

Even if this observation is accurate, it is surely based on a questionable theology. When congregations cease to rely upon an outside subsidy and look instead to their own resources for ministry, they can make theological as well as economic discoveries. The priesthood of all believers can become not just a theory but a reality.[28]

5

Inevitably the strategy proposed for Churches in *Faith in the Countryside* is slanted towards the Church of England. Yet there are, I believe, lessons that can be learned for Churches more widely from the report. It is apposite that it should have considered the needs of rural England. Localised ecology is at present one of the most persistent ethical issues in the secular world. And rural congregations are often intimately involved in this wider concern.

Furthermore, Religion, Earth and Creation have extensive, and perhaps even natural, links. *Faith in the Countryside* has responded to some of these links. By starting from the theme of Creation, they have responded in part to what Sean McDonagh identifies as the '*kairos*' facing the Churches. Writing very recently on the theme of 'The Greening of the Church', he maintains:

> 'In the Christian context this is a crisis or *kairos*-filled moment. The events unfolding in front of our eyes call for a choice between living in a way that enhances all life or continuing to hurtle down the road to disaster. The crisis is heightened by the realisation that this generation of people is in a unique position in relation to all other generations who have lived

[28] See my *Beyond Decline*, op. cit.

before us and those who will live in the future. We received the blessings of a healthy natural world with clean air and water, fertile soil and an abundance of life – a world in full flower. The decisions taken now will determine whether we will hand on this precious heritage intact to our children or whether we will irreversibly destroy earth's fruitfulness. Ensuring that we do the latter is surely the religious task of this generation of Christians.'[29]

However, sadly *Faith in the Countryside* has shown little of the hard-headedness that ought to characterise attempts at Christian ethics in secular worlds. It is not sufficient to grasp the empirical issues. Sustained moral and theological connections must also be made – a far more difficult task. And Churches themselves should be challenged in ways that grasp both their long-standing problems and their presently unleashed potentialities. Considerably more ploughing is needed.

[29] Sean McDonagh, *The Greening of the Church*, Chapman and Orbis 1990, pp. 5–6.

4

From Progress to Survival

In the last chapter the focus was upon localised ecology. In this chapter I will take a broader look at two of the central concepts – namely 'progress' and 'survival' – that have been used over the years in discussions of macro-ecology. If once people tended to regard technology as unambiguously beneficial and as a sign of human 'progress', today there is a widespread ambivalence towards technology. We strongly desire the fruits of technology – transport systems, communications systems, entertainment systems, and so forth – yet we fear their long-term ecological consequences. Fears of global warming, industrial pollution, and nuclear holocaust, effected directly or indirectly by ever-advancing technology, have caused many to become increasingly pessimistic about the long-term survival of mankind. A complex and little understood system of global self-regulation seems endangered by technological 'progress'. In short, ecological ethics has shifted from pride in 'progress' to fears about 'survival'.

This shift in perception can be illustrated by comparing T. H. Huxley's Victorian social optimism with more recent attitudes towards technology. In his celebrated lecture on 'Evolution and Ethics' of 1893 Huxley argued:

> 'Let us understand, once for all, that the ethical progress of society depends, not on imitating the cosmic process, still less in running away from it, but in combating it. It may seem an audacious proposal thus to pit the microcosm against the macrocosm and to set man to subdue nature to his higher ends; but I venture to think that the great intellectual difference between the ancient times ... and our day, lies in the solid foundation we have acquired for the hope that

such an enterprise may meet with a certain measure of success.'[1]

Huxley was no euphoric utopian. He was equally concerned to criticise contemporary pessimism as evolutionary optimism, pointing out that cosmic evolution might well be cyclical. For him the state of the cosmos was 'the expression of a transitory adjustment of contending forces; a scene of strife, in which all the combatants fall in turn',[2] human beings included.

Nevertheless, he was a firm believer in the essentially progressive nature of contemporary technology, and it was on the basis of this belief that he derived an ethical stance. Huxley was convinced that 'as civilisation has advanced, so has the extent of this interference increased; until the organised and highly developed sciences and arts of the present day have endowed man with a command over the course of non-human nature greater than that once attributed to the magicians. The most impressive, I might say startling, of these changes have been brought about in the course of the last two centuries; while a right comprehension of the process of life and of the means of influencing its manifestations is only just dawning upon us'.[3]

It would be hard to find parallels to Huxley's optimism about the effects of technology amongst contemporary writers. The dangerous, and possibly fatal, societal and ecological effects of technology seem all too apparent, and there is a growing literature on the subject. In this chapter I will attempt to chart some of the implications for Christian ethics in secular worlds that have resulted from this change of perspective on the effects of technology.

I

The very concept of 'progress', as distinct from 'change', is ethically based. Huxley was not just asserting that contemporary technology effects 'changes' in nature, nor that this technology simply generates 'new insights', but that these changes are

[1] T. H. Huxley, *Evolution and Ethics and Other Essays*, London 1894, p. 83.
[2] ibid., p. 49.
[3] ibid., p. 84.

'better' than the status quo, and that the 'new insights' are 'better insights'. He gave few clues about why this should be so or about the basis of his value-judgements. Nevertheless it is clear that for him it was so.

By 1927 J. S. Huxley had certainly modified the views of his grandfather, yet he still held an implicit belief in the essentially progressive nature of contemporary science and technology:

> 'Industrialism, education, science, and communications, topped by the War, have brought the forces of change to a head, and the time is ripe. The moment does indeed seem to be approaching when man can and should begin constructing a new common outlook, a new habitation for his spirit, new from the foundations up, on the basis of scientific humanism. The eighteenth century attempted it, but failed. Reason was not enough; more of brute fact and fact's control was needed. Nor was it enough that Reason should shine in the few; education and social reconstruction were also necessary, and so the age of Reason gave way, through wars and revolutions, to the age of Science and Industry.'[4]

Today even Huxley's call for a renewed spirit of science, tinged with the spirit of a non-transcendent religion, is likely to be greeted with scepticism. In chapter 6 it will be seen that the non-theism of Don Cupitt shares none of Huxley's confidence about the benefits of science. The spectres of nuclear warfare and environmental pollution have shaken the faith of many in science and technology. His non-transcendent religion has been attempted with little apparent success. And even his implicit belief in 'facts' is by no means shared by all.[5]

It is significant that a present-day defender of a Christian understanding of 'progress', A. G. B. Woollard,[6] makes little mention of technological progress. In fact he criticises theologians, such as Harvey Cox in his book *The Secular City*[7] for their naive optimism about the essentially progressive nature of contemporary science and technology (a criticism that Cox

[4] J. S. Huxley, *Religion Without Revelation*, London 1927, pp. 8–9.
[5] See Liam Hudson, *The Cult of the Fact*, Jonathan Cape 1972.
[6] A. G. B. Woollard, *Progress: A Christian Doctrine?*, SPCK 1972.
[7] Harvey Cox, *The Secular City: Urbanisation and Secularisation in Theological Perspective*, Macmillan and SCM Press 1965.

himself now acknowledges[8]). Instead, Woollard can only provide meaning for the term 'progress' from Process theology (mixed with insights from the Catholic Left concerning persons-in-community). His is an essentially theistic understanding of 'progress':

> 'This evolving universe in its complexity points to the need for a Principle of unity in which all things can be held together in dynamic tension, which can evoke and maintain the universal thrust towards creativity and newness. Such a Principle, being the highest Reality of all, must exhibit at least these qualities of personality, self-consciousness, and purpose-fulness which come to their fruition in man. Hence this Principle . . . can rightly be called "God".'[9]

Further, there is nothing 'automatic' about this understanding of Process theology. Woollard maintains that, as in Teilhard de Chardin,[10] there is 'the possibility of an ultimate "opting out" of a whole section of the creation which refuses to co-operate in the achievement of the goal'.[11] Within this overall context of Process theology Woollard believes that social ethics assumes a new role:

> 'It would be bound to pay great regard, more than traditional Christian ethics has ever done, to the witness of the natural and social sciences. It cannot divide "what is" and "what ought to be" as rigidly in its thought as Hume and the whole secular tradition has done. The "is", as revealed by empirical study, points to the "ought", as its "depth dimensions" are seen by those who have vision. It is not of course identical with the ought; certainly not in the shallow sense that "all men ought to do what most men actually do" . . . The relationship between "is" and "ought" lies at a deeper level; that of the discovery of the "true nature of man".'[12]

Woollard's spirited attempt to uphold the notion of 'progress', albeit in this much changed form, faces a number of crucial difficulties. In the first place, it must face all the usual criticisms

[8] See Harvey Cox, *Religion in the Secular City: Toward a Postmodern Theology*, Simon and Schuster 1984.
[9] op. cit., p. 57.
[10] P. Teilhard de Chardin, *The Phenomenon of Man*, Fontana 1959.
[11] op. cit., p. 64.
[12] op. cit., p. 58.

that are made of Process theology, which Woollard admits but does not explore. Amongst these criticisms is the questionability of jumping from notions of biological evolution to notions of social evolution. Secondly, Woollard's formulation does not altogether escape the 'automatic' charge that is frequently made. So, it is often argued today that Teilhard de Chardin – so popular in the 1960s – only allows for the possibility of a section of the creation 'opting out', not for the whole creation 'opting out'. For Teilhard de Chardin, although the universe becomes increasingly complex, it nonetheless has an ultimate tendency towards 'convergent integration'. For John Polkinghorne, in complete contrast, its ultimate tendency is rather towards disintegration.[13] But for Woollard such a total 'opting out' in the context of Process theology would be tantamount to a disproof of God's existence. Finally, his formulation of the role of social ethics, *vis-a-vis* Process theology, depends on a discovery of the 'true nature of man' – a task which might prove as difficult as that of Bultmann's search for 'authentic man'.

2

The role of social ethics changes drastically amongst those whose focus of attention is on 'survival' rather than on 'progress'. Ethical writers who are concerned with the survival of mankind in the contemporary world, might perhaps be divided into two classes, although of course a single writer may well combine both characteristics. In the first class are those who are primarily concerned with the physical survival of mankind. The focus of these writers is upon the ecological implications of contemporary technology, and they are concerned with the ethical implications of the possibility that life for mankind on this planet is shortly to end unless drastic steps can be taken to limit and then to reduce technology.

On the other hand, there are those writers who are more concerned with the survival of 'mankind as mankind'. They tend to be concerned with the potentially destructive aspects of contemporary technology which have the capacity (it is held) to

[13] John Polkinghorne, *Science and Providence: God's Interaction with the World*, SPCK 1989, p.95.

'dehumanise' human beings. Amongst these writers it is commonly held that a dependence upon technology and upon the fruits of technology involves an increasing loss of human 'freedom', instead of the 'work-free', 'leisured' life-style once envisaged by some socialist utopians.

The first class is not comprised solely of prophets of doom. It is significant that I. G. Barbour, who is both a supporter of Process theology and a critic of the 'pessimists who advocate a halt to scientific development',[14] is well aware of the ecological dangers inherent in contemporary technology. In fact his basic concern when examining the ethics of technology has for long been to call for a 'redirection' of this technology:

> 'The redirection of technology, in sum, is the crucial challenge of this decade. Man can still decide his future before it is too late. He can act to fulfil the promise: "Earth shall be fair, and all her people one". Technology can yet be man's servant rather than his master.'[15]

There is no conviction in Barbour's writings that mankind in fact will fulfil this promise: he only states that mankind could still fulfil it. The very fervour of his plea for a redirection of technology, indicates at least a concern about the current directions of technology – a concern, that is, for the survival of human beings. Yet his support of Process theology appears to be less central to his social ethics than that of Woollard. Indeed, in his recent Gifford lectures he acknowledges that 'process' is but one partial model (albeit for him the best) to depict God's relationship to the world:

> 'All models are limited and partial, and none gives a complete or adequate picture of reality. The world is diverse, and differing aspects of it indeed may be better represented by one model than by another. God's relation to persons will differ from God's relation to impersonal objects like stars and rocks. The pursuit of coherence must not lead us to neglect such differences. We need diverse models to remind us of these differences.'[16]

[14] Ian G. Barbour, *Science and Secularity: The Ethics of Technology*, SCM Press 1970, p. 74.

[15] ibid., p. 142.

[16] Ian G. Barbour, *Religion in an Age of Science*, SCM Press 1990, p. 270.

The second class of writer has included such different scholars as Jacques Ellul[17] and the celebrated, but much criticised,[18] Herbert Marcuse.[19] Ellul forcefully outlined the 'depersonalising' and 'dehumanising' character of a society shaped by technology. He argued that, because of the uniform nature of contemporary culture, resulting from such phenomena as the mass media and mass production, differences between individuals and groups tend to disappear. Marcuse's metaphysical assumptions were very different from those of Ellul, but his conclusions were remarkably similar. For him contemporary technology in the West has produced a thoroughly 'one dimensional society', a society essentially lacking in 'freedom'. Marcuse believed that increasing 'mechanisation' and 'standardisation', themselves effects of technology, far from liberating human beings from want, have in fact created a society without any effective critical opposition:

> 'A comfortable, smooth, reasonable, democratic unfreedom prevails in advanced industrial civilisation, a token of technical progress ... The rights and liberties which were such vital factors in the origins and earlier stages of industrial society yield to a higher stage of this society; they are losing their traditional rationale and content. Freedom of thought, speech, and conscience were – just as free enterprise, which they served to promote and protect – essentially critical ideas, designed to replace an obsolescent material and intellectual culture by a more productive and rational one. Once institutionalised, these rights and liberties shared the fate of the society of which they had become an integral part. The achievement cancels the premises.'[20]

Both of these prophetic writers of the 1960s suffered from similar weaknesses. Firstly, both were inclined to make seemingly empirical generalisations about the effects of technology without a detailed analysis of empirical data.[21] Secondly, both showed a sense of nostalgia for a 'humanity' or 'humanness' that mankind

[17] Jacques Ellul, *The Technological Society*, London 1964.
[18] See Alasdair MacIntyre, *Marcuse*, Fontana 1970.
[19] Herbert Marcuse, *One-Dimensional Man*, Boston 1964 and Sphere Books 1968.
[20] ibid., p. 19.
[21] cf. MacIntyre, op. cit.

is supposed to have lost. Just as Marshall McLuhan,[22] at the time, looked longingly away from contemporary technological society dominated by the mass media and back to what he termed 'tribal man', so both Ellul and Marcuse shared an implicit belief in what is 'really', or perhaps even 'authentically', human. Strangely they were all subject, in their view of social ethics, to the same criticism as Woollard, despite starting from differing premises. It is easy enough to use such terms as 'depersonalising' and 'dehumanising', and at first they appear to have meaning, yet it is far more difficult to elucidate, and then substantiate, them.

This final point proved particularly troublesome at the time. In the context of a debate about world development, David Jenkins exposed some of the pit-falls involved. In an essay in an influential symposium in the early 1970s, *Technology and Social Justice*, written whilst he was still at the World Council of Churches, Jenkins questioned the current search for 'the human' in world development:

> 'Although "seeking to obtain the human" or "being concerned with humanisation" or "making a central issue of the criteria of the human" sound important and significant, what do phrases of this nature in fact mean? They do not directly reflect the facts of the varying situations to be met with in countries of the "third world" or in blacks struggling against the effects of white racism or in youth protests. They represent rather the reflections and judgements of certain persons or classes about those situations, struggles and protests. These situations and struggles are described as having a significance, a context, an aim beyond themselves and the assumption is that this is a common significance, context and aim.'[23]

Jenkins had little faith in 'generalities' and 'abstractions'.[24] Nevertheless, he still advanced the following concept of 'the human':

> 'It is the development of, use of and responsibility for science and technology which is that which is distinctly human.'[25]

---

[22] Marshall McLuhan, *The Medium is the Message*, Penguin 1967.
[23] David E. Jenkins in R. H. Preston (ed), *Technology and Social Justice*, SCM Press 1971, p. 209.
[24] ibid., p. 211.
[25] ibid., p. 213.

He claimed at the time that this was not 'related to vague abstractions called "values" but to precisely delimited and organised particulars which constitute the facts of the case'.[26] So this was not advanced as a part of some quest for the 'really human'. Unfortunately such a qualification tends to empty the concept of much of its meaning. The concept becomes little more than a map-reference, albeit perhaps a useful map-reference.

3

The distinctions drawn so far need not be seen as mutually exclusive. Rather my aim has been to draw attention to certain distinguishable focuses, and to point to some of the weaknesses that they tend to face. So, to claim that within the field of social ethics in the context of the effects of technology, there is a minority of writers whose focus of attention is still on concepts of 'progress' and a majority whose focus is on 'survival', and that within the latter group there are those who are basically concerned with physical survival and others who are concerned with a qualitative survival, is not to claim that these are exclusive focuses of attention.

The seminal document of the early 1970s *A Blueprint For Survival* well illustrates this. Sheer physical survival was clearly paramount in its analysis of the disruption of ecosystems, failure of food supplies, exhaustion of resources and the collapse of society. The document stated unambiguously:

> 'The principal defect of the industrial way of life with its ethos of expansion is that it is not sustainable. Its termination within the lifetime of someone born today is inevitable – unless it continues to be sustained for a while longer by an entrenched minority at the cost of imposing great suffering on the rest of mankind.'[27]

This preliminary analysis was immediately followed by detailed proposals on ecology, conservation and population-growth, showing how radical changes might effect mankind's physical survival in this world. Gradually it emerged however, that

[26] ibid., p. 213.
[27] *A Blueprint for Survival*, first published in *The Economist*, January 1972, para. 110.

qualitative judgements about survival were also being employed in the document. So, for example, it argued:

> 'Man in our present society has been deprived of a satisfactory social environment. A society made up of decentralised, self-sufficient communities, in which people work near their homes, have the responsibility of governing themselves, of running their schools, hospitals, and welfare services, in fact of constituting real communities, should, we feel, be a much happier place. Its members, in these conditions, would be likely to develop an identity of their own, which many of us have lost in the mass society we live in.'[28]

This passage is reminiscent, albeit in a modified form, of Ellul and Marcuse. Contemporary technology was thought to effect certain qualitative changes in human life. But at least in this context the claim was supported by clear references to empirical data. Yet it is important to realise that it was still a value claim, depending more upon certain implicit values than upon this empirical data.

Further, it is possible that this claim contained an implicit notion of 'progress'. Of course this was not the same notion as that of T. H. Huxley. The latter's optimism about science and technology had gone. Nor did there appear to be an implicit evolutionary theory here. Yet the proposed future state was clearly thought to be 'better' than the present state, and, in so far as this is true, then *A Blueprint for Survival* was concerned with 'progress' and not simply with 'change'. This is evident even more clearly in the following statement:

> 'In a stable society, everything would be done to reduce the discrepancy between economic value and real value, and if we could repair some of the damage we have done to our physical and social environment, and live a more natural life, there would be less need for the consumer products that we spend so much money on. Instead we could spend it on things that truly enrich and embellish our lives.'[29]

Three words in the two sentences are particularly significant: 'real', 'natural', and 'truly'. Again, as used in these sentences,

[28] ibid., para. 345.
[29] ibid., para. 345.

they are strangely reminiscent of the term 'authentic'. They have transformed a seemingly empirical statement into a value statement. For the ethicist this may be both heartening and perplexing; heartening to find that values were still considered important, but perplexing to know which values were in fact being used. References in *A Blueprint for Survival* to 'satisfaction' and 'happiness' would seem to suggest that some form of pragmatism was implicit. However, references to such notions as 'more natural' would seem to imply something quite different.

A second document at the time, *Sinews For Survival*, also showed a value-laden approach to 'survival'. It too was primarily concerned with physical survival:

> 'It must be apparent that we are by no means complacent about the management of natural resources in Britain or in the world. We are unhappy about the implications of yet more intensive farming technology and the impact of monocultural forestry; about the threats to fish stocks by man's use of the ocean as a sink; about the reduction in diversity of wildlife as our human requirements become more pervasive; about the enormous scale of the need for public expenditure on the elimination of river pollution; about the supply of some sedimentary minerals and their effect on the environment; about the growth of demand for energy and the environmental effects of its supply; about the imperious demands of the motor car and its consequences for the quality of life. Above all, we doubt whether our many misgivings can be overcome unless our human population is stabilised. There is not much time to spare.'[30]

For some even this approach to the issue of physical survival will appear too optimistic, despite the list of areas mentioned. To them the word 'misgivings' might appear too weak. Yet within this passage a qualitative approach is also evident, as the crucial words 'quality of life' indicate. This approach was even more apparent elsewhere in the document:

> 'What we need is to stand high in the table of useful growth: growth that removes poverty and squalor and aids human fulfilment; growth that emphasises quality and rejects shoddi-

[30] *Sinews for Survival*, HMSO 1972, para. 192.

ness. We need a better way of defining the kinds of growth we need. And, in the longer term, just as we need to plan to bring our population into balance with what the environment can support, so we need to plan for economic stability at a level that provides the environmental conditions and quality of life that we would wish for ourselves and our children.'[31]

Here too the initial value term 'useful' suggests that a pragmatic approach of one sort or another was being adopted. Yet the introduction of the terms 'fulfilment' and 'quality of life' suggest quite different ethical assumptions.

In both documents it is possible that the sort of uneasy tension between pragmatism and principles mentioned in the Introduction lies at the heart of this ethical ambivalence. Scientists, management specialists and social scientists appear to be internally divided on what might be seen as moral issues. For some there are at stake issues of deep principle which involve individuals inescapably in the Niebuhrian tension between 'moral man and immoral society'. For others moral issues, if they are to be identified as 'moral' at all, are to be resolved by essentially pragmatic means.

4

If my analysis is correct, then it should be apparent that there is considerable confusion in much of the literature on the effects of contemporary technology in the area of social ethics. It is a confusion that results partly from a tension between differing approaches and partly from the use of unexplained value terms.

But how should the theologian respond? In the 1960s the theologian Ian Ramsey[32] argued for a modified natural law approach which sought consensus between Christians and others on the basis of shared values derived initially from the belief that it is good to survive. A generation later Stanley Hauerwas argues for a more distinctly theological approach stressing the dissimilarity between Christian attitudes towards physical survival and secular aspirations for global survival. Together they well illustrate the two quite distinct approaches, which have already been noted at several points in this book, in attempts to do

---

[31] ibid., para. 16.
[32] I. T. Ramsey, *Christian Ethics and Contemporary Philosophy*, SCM Press 1966.

Christian ethics in secular worlds. They might easily be regarded as mutually incompatible. I believe instead that both are valid ways of doing Christian ethics in secular worlds, albeit ways appropriate for quite different audiences.

The Ramsey approach was deliberately intended to act as a bridge between differing communities. It sought agreement between both the theologically committed and the theologically uncommitted around a shared belief that it is good to survive. This minimalist approach to ethics started from brute physical survival and only proceeded tentatively to qualitative survival. It observed that most people (whether they have any religious convictions or not) do believe that physical survival is 'desirable' and even 'good'. Further, they usually continue to believe this even in situations of extreme difficulty and pain. Doubtless there have always been advocates of suicide and euthanasia: yet they have seldom if ever constituted a majority in any population, even in a population experiencing chaos or catastrophe. What Durkheim termed anomic suicide[33] is by no means a common phenomenon. That being the case an obvious question arises: Why is it good to survive as a human being in this world? And answers to this question frequently postulate that human life has some intrinsic or extrinsic value. Thus value judgements may be implicit within the beliefs about survival that characterise most human beings.

Hauerwas presents a stark contrast to this way of doing Christian ethics in secular worlds. He frequently rejects such arguments – which he variously identifies as 'secular' or 'liberal' – and contrasts them with explicitly theological arguments. So, when discussing the ethics of suicide, he questions the dominant presumption that 'the prohibition of suicide is grounded in our "natural desire to live" ... The very phrase "natural desire to live" is fraught with ambiguity, but, even worse, it seems to suggest that when a person no longer has such a desire there is no longer any reason for living'.[34] For Hauerwas then:

[33] Emile Durkheim, *Suicide: A Study in Sociology*, 1897, and Routledge and Kegan Paul 1952.
[34] Stanley Hauerwas, *Suffering Presence: Theological Reflections on Medicine, the Mentally Handicapped, and the Church*, University of Notre Dame 1986 and T&T Clark 1988, pp. 105-6.

'In contrast, the language of gift does not presuppose we have "a natural desire to live", but rather that our living is an obligation. It is an obligation that we at once owe our Creator and one another. For our creaturely status is but a reminder that our existence is not secured by our own power, but rather requires the constant care of, and trust in, others. Our willingness to live in the face of suffering, pain, and sheer boredom of life is morally a service to one another as it is a sign that life can be endured and moreover our living can be done with joy and exuberance.'[35]

These positions are clearly different from each other, but are they actually mutually incompatible? Theists might wish to encourage non-theists to hold the first argument, whilst still believing that it is the second which is the more satisfactory. They might even interpret some assumed 'natural desire to live' as an intimation of creatureliness. Such an approach would certainly accord quite closely to classic natural arguments. Even if, following Chapter 1, Christian ethicists are often sceptical about our ability to discern what is 'natural', the continuities between secular and Christian forms of ethics presupposed by natural law theorists remain an important option. Without this broad option Christian ethics might soon become little more than a ghetto activity.

This is not, of course, to assume that secular and Christian forms of ethics will always be mutually compatible. Christians may well find that there are some approaches, assumptions or even contexts that are genuinely incompatible. But it is to assume that continuities between Christianity and society at large are usually worth serious and sustained exploration. Christian ethics in secular worlds is not simply about proclamation and denunciation (although these will sometimes be necessary, especially in evil regimes[36]). It is more often about listening, about patient exploration and about attempting to show that Christian ethics adds depth to perceptions that may already be present within an apparently secular world.

Another contrast that Hauerwas makes elsewhere is between

---

[35] ibid., p. 106.
[36] See further my *Beyond Decline*, SCM Press 1988.

what he terms 'survivalist' objections to nuclear weapons and more specifically Christian objections (whether from the just war or the pacifist tradition):

> 'In contrast to pacifists and just war advocates, the survivalists do not begin with an established theory about if and when life can be taken justly. Rather survivalists are so impressed with the destructive power of nuclear weapons and a sense of horror with the prospect of their use they conclude nuclear war must be excluded at all costs. Their concern is not whether nuclear weapons can be used in a discriminating manner, but whether the very existence of such weapons does not threaten the existence of the human species . . . They do so by condemning nuclear weapons not because they cannot be used in a discriminating manner but because they threaten the existence of the globe. So survivalists have an interest in maintaining that nuclear war will be total war since otherwise they would have no basis for singling out nuclear weapons as deserving particular condemnation.'[37]

Those starting from a specifically Christian tradition will, so Hauerwas maintains, argue quite differently. For them 'life cannot be an end in and of itself – there are many things for which we should be willing to die rather than lose these goods. For example, we should be willing to sacrifice much, perhaps even our lives, rather than abandon the innocent to violent destruction'.[38]

But here, too, it is not obvious that these positions are mutually incompatible. The survivalist argument is based upon global destruction, not upon the destruction of individuals. And few Christians look upon global destruction favourably. Doubtless they do so for rather different reasons from those offered by the survivalist, but they might nonetheless still take the latter's reasons seriously, without regarding them as self-sufficient. The Thomistic maxim that grace crowns nature works quite well here. Christian ethics does change some of the rhetoric of survivalists – especially claims to the effect that this life is all that there is – and it adds to it a context of God's creative love, but it

[37] Stanley Hauerwas, *Against the Nations: War and Survival in a Liberal Society*, Winston Press 1985, pp. 140–1.
[38] ibid., p. 154.

can still affirm its ecological seriousness and its faith that life is deeply endowed with value. These secular perceptions are not denounced, but affirmed and transfigured.

Here, I believe, it is possible to see how these two quite different ways of doing Christian ethics in secular worlds, characterised so differently by Ramsey and Hauerwas, are mutually compatible and valid. Again, this is not to claim that this will always be so. But where it is so Christian ethicists would be ill advised to abandon dialogue with secular worlds. Human survival and ecological concerns manifestly cross intellectual and faith boundaries. And it is perhaps a duty of Christians to explore these boundaries, to listen, to learn, and only then to prompt or challenge.

5

Fabricated Man –
Twenty Years On

Some of the most challenging ethical issues concerning ecology are currently being raised by biotechnology. This fast moving secular world presents Christian ethics with a series of bewildering dilemmas. And, as mentioned in the Introduction, genetic scientists themselves are internally divided on many of these ethical dilemmas. What is possible to do now, or what might be possible to do one day, may or may not be what ought to be done. Biotechnology presents a complex spectrum of scientific innovation, futuristic dreams, and perhaps even apocalyptic nightmares.

One of the earliest Christian ethicists to explore the implications of biotechnology was the late Paul Ramsey. Here *par excellence* was the exponent of Christian ethics in secular worlds. And some twenty years ago he wrote his most imaginative and speculative book – *Fabricated Man: The Ethics of Genetic Control*.[1] The work is clearly a product of the 1960s. The generic use of the term 'man' is sufficient to indicate that. But so is the humanistic optimism of the scientists that Ramsey reviewed. In the book Ramsey himself was manifestly at the height of his shrewd but bombastic skills.

The work is a *tour de force*, challenging those engaged in genetic biotechnology to face up to the ethical and religious implications of their work and of the direction that it might take. By this stage Ramsey had inherited some of the mantle of Reinhold Niebuhr as the most powerful Protestant voice in

[1] Paul Ramsey, *Fabricated Man: The Ethics of Genetic Control*, Yale University Press, New Haven and London, 1970.

Christian ethics. Like Niebuhr he was listened to in America by both theological and non-theological audiences. Without ever attaining the full stature of Niebuhr, especially in the political sphere, he combined a strong desire for empirical accuracy with a penchant for prophetic theology. *Fabricated Man* shows him, I believe, at his best. It is a fearless, witty and sophisticated little book which seeks to challenge growing scientific orthodoxies – or, more accurately, the growing moral orthodoxies of scientists – whilst listening to the empirical actualities and possibilities of the new biology. He did not pretend to be a scientist – any more than I do myself – but rather saw himself as an interested layman who was also a professional ethicist and theologian.

Because *Fabricated Man* illustrates so well one way of doing Christian ethics in a secular world (and its limitations), I will set out Ramsey's arguments at some length before criticising them. The criticisms that I will offer will be of two sorts; first empirical criticisms which I have been able to glean from qualified scientists and then ethical and theological criticisms which signal my divergences from his critique.

After twenty years it will not be surprising to find that some of the empirical data have changed. Doubtless in twenty years time, given the rapid developments that are taking place in bio-technology, they will have changed again. As a result the stock of ethical and theological resources that are deployed in the debate may vary somewhat – with some resources becoming more or less appropriate in the new empirical situation. However, for the most part my differences from Ramsey will result, more from our differing perceptions of which resources were appropriate then and especially from our differing approaches to Christian in secular worlds, than from the empirical changes that have taken place over the last twenty years.

I

Ramsey's analysis started from the genetic dilemma caused by advances in general and reproductive medicine. As doctors become more skilled in helping those with genetic defects to survive into maturity, and then in helping them once mature to reproduce, so he believed there would be an 'exponential increase' in the prevalence of such defects within the general population. For example, the genetic defect which causes diabetes invariably resulted before insulin in an early death – thus ensuring that its level did not greatly increase in the population at large. Even after the discovery of insulin diabetic women tended to miscarry. Today, however, with further medical advances in carefully controlling diabetics, women with the disorder can both reach maturity and reproduce – ensuring in the process that this genetic defect will become more and more widespread. If this scenario is then replicated across a range, indeed a growing range, of conditions caused by genetic defects, the long-term prospect for human beings, in Ramsey's opinion, looks increasingly bleak.

Although Ramsey did not express it in quite these terms, modern medicine arguably is creating a situation for human beings which is the reverse of Darwinian evolution. If for Darwin nature is characterised by the survival of the fittest, modern medicine seems committed to the principle of enabling the weakest to survive and then to reproduce. Viewed in biological terms this can only result, if unchecked, in an ever-decreasingly healthy species. Statistically, after only a few generations genetic defects will become rampant. Unlike generally avoidable infections such as AIDS – to which I shall return in the final Chapter – endemic genetic defects will result from the normal functions of modern medicine and monogamous reproduction. It even feeds on the most decent of human sympathies; the desire to help the afflicted and the desire to enable the infertile to have children. Yet it may eventually prove even more destructive for human beings than AIDS might. And its social control will be considerably more difficult than that of AIDS.

This *is* an ethical dilemma which is too frequently ignored – even if Ramsey's language might now appear too alarmist. His *Fabricated Man* sets it out starkly in all of its ethical complexity. Or rather, he sets out in great detail the range of options that human beings have for containing this dilemma alongside the ethical and theological resources that seem appropriate to them. It is the aim of his book to sift through these complex options, to encourage the adoption of some and to warn against others.

Manifestly these options raise ethical and sometimes political questions. Ramsey was quite sure that they should not simply be left to the scientific or medical communities to decide. As with AIDS today, if forms of social control, positive or negative, are required to prevent general genetic deterioration, then society as a whole is involved. It is no longer an issue just for the empirical experts. And even if forms of genetic intervention are adopted as a means of control, ethical issues may be raised which also affect the whole community. Genetic surgery or genetic engineering may have risks for our present and future which are properly the concern for scientists and non-scientists alike. Once this much is established then the role of the ethicist or theologian in this admittedly technical and often speculative area becomes more evident. He or she does have a relevant expertise, albeit an expertise which must listen carefully to medical biotechnologists.

Ramsey considered three broad options for controlling genetic degeneration. The first of these – passive control – relies upon genetic counselling to encourage those at risk not to have children. He rejected out of hand any attempt to coerce those at risk and, like most of those involved in the debate, insisted that passive control must be voluntary. The second – active control – relies upon recent biotechnology, in the form of AID (artificial insemination by donor), egg or embryo donation, or, in its most futuristic form, cloning, to by-pass the semen or ova of those with genetic defects. The third – biochemical, viral or micro-surgical control – uses futuristic techniques, such as genetic surgery, chemical agencies or specially tailored viruses, actually to correct genetic defects. Ramsey's ethical and theological objections were overwhelmingly directed at the second of these broad options. He was happy with the techniques envisaged in the third – provided that they could be achieved without unethical side-effects. However, since these techniques remain just speculative possibilities, the option that he commended for the present is the first.

Passive, voluntary control, then, was held to be the only current ethical way of ensuring that human beings do not suffer from increasing genetic deterioration as a result of scientific and medical advances. Dissenting from traditionalist Catholics, Ramsey argued that 'if there are reasons for the systematic and lifelong practice of birth control (already a conclusion reached by

Catholic moral theology), and if serious genetic defect finds a place among the reasons grave enough to warrant having no children at all, or no more children, then vasectomy would seem to be in principle permissible, perhaps commendable, maybe morally obligatory'.[2] Sterilisation must always be voluntary, but it is entirely legitimate and praiseworthy for those at risk.

Yet Ramsey was aware that passive control may not actually be very effective in preventing long-term genetic deterioration. Couples even knowing of some grave risk are frequently prepared nonetheless to have children. Their urge to reproduce seems to overcome prudential considerations that might result from genetic counselling. It is precisely at this point that he argued for an enlarging of the moral vision – to include an 'ethics of genetic duty' – through specifically Christian resources:

> 'What is lacking is not the moral argument but a moral movement. The Christian churches have in the past been able to promote celibacy to the glory of God – men and women who for the supreme end of human existence "deny themselves" (if that is the term for it) both of the goods of marriage. These same Christian churches should be able to promote voluntary or "vocational" childlessness, or politics of restricted reproduction, for the sake of the children of generations to come . . . the churches could set before such couples alternatives that might be termed "foster parentage" – all the many ways in which human parental instincts may be fulfilled in couples who for mercy's sake have no children of their own. These persons would be called upon to "deny themselves" (if that is the term for it) one of the goods of marriage for the sake of that end itself. And they would honour the Creator of all human love and procreation, in that they would hold in incorruptible union the love that they have and the procreation they never have, or have no more.'[3]

2

Twenty years later, with AID, egg donation, and techniques dependent upon IVF (in vitro fertilisation) so widespread and with the moral debate centring more upon surrogacy and fetal

[2] *F.M.*, p. 43.
[3] *F.M.*, p. 59.

experimentation, it may seem surprising that Ramsey categorically rejected active forms of genetic control. For many it might seem obvious that if genetic defects are not to be increased then couples at risk should be encouraged to have children through biotechnological means. Whilst the spectre of cloning – parthenogenesis or androgenesis – might evoke very considerable moral reservations amongst many, Ramsey's non-Catholic rejection of active means *in toto* might seem somewhat idiosyncratic.

However, *Fabricated Man* insisted that couples do not have a right to have children, and certainly not a right to have children through morally unacceptable means. And Ramsey concluded that the means adopted in active forms of genetic control *are* morally unacceptable.

His arguments here form the very heart of the challenge of *Fabricated Man* and also demonstrate the gulf he saw between liberal humanism and Judaeo–Christian ethics. His were in essence theological arguments and his approach, although characterised by numerous contacts with scientists, was more akin (on the lines set out in the last chapter) to that of Stanley Hauerwas today than to that of his contemporary and namesake Ian Ramsey.

At several points in his analysis Paul Ramsey signalled his dislike of mechanistic understandings of human sexuality and what he termed the 'atomistic individualism' of prevailing scientific attitudes. He preferred the term 'procreation' to the mechanistic term 'reproduction'.[4] He ridiculed some of the more fanciful speculations about the function of human or part-human clones (e.g. legless people for extended space travel!). He contrasted Christian attitudes towards monogamous marriage and parenthood with more functional attitudes which regard such family relationships as 'guilty of monopoly'. And he juxtaposed the malleable vision of the world held by some secular scientists with the Jewish and Christian understandings of the world as created order:

> 'Men and women are created in covenant, to covenant, and for covenant. Creation is *toward* the love of Christ. Christians,

---

[4] cf. B. K. Rothman, 'The Products of Conception: the Social Context of Reproductive Choices', *Journal of Medical Ethics*, 1985, 11, 188–92.

therefore, will not readily admit that the energies of sex, for example, have any other primary *telos*, another final end, than Jesus Christ. Rather they will find in the strength of human sexual passion (beyond the obvious needs of procreation) an evident *telos* of acts of sexual love toward making real the meaning of man-womanhood, nurturing covenant-love between the parties, fostering their care for one another, prefiguring Christ's love for the Church – whatever other substrata of purposes sexual energy may have that can be discovered by intending the world as a biologist. And in human procreativity out of the depths of human sexual love is prefigured God's own act of creation out of the profound mystery of his love revealed in Christ. To put radically asunder what God joined together in parenthood when He made love procreative, to procreate from beyond the sphere of love (AID, for example, or making human life in a test-tube), or to posit acts of sexual love beyond the sphere of responsible procreation (by definition, marriage), means a refusal of the image of God's creation in our own.'[5]

This theological understanding of human sexuality had obvious points in common with the traditional Catholic view, examined in Chapter 1, which was enshrined so decisively, two years before *Fabricated Man* was published, in *Humanae Vitae*.[6] Both saw sexuality as created by God with unitive and procreative ends and both insisted that these ends could not legitimately be divided. For Ramsey, though, 'this does not mean that sexual intercourse always in fact nourishes love between the parties or always engenders a child. It simply means that it *tends*, of its own nature, toward the strengthening of love (the unitive or the communicative good), and toward the engendering of children (the procreative good)'.[7]

He was aware that some uses of Natural Law in this area in Catholic moral theology make it very difficult to justify sexual intercourse between those who know they are sterile or who are past childbearing age. In contrast, he insisted that we must

[5] *F.M.*, pp. 38–9.
[6] Pope Paul VI's Encyclical Letter *Humanae Vitae*, Catholic Truth Society, London, 1968.
[7] *F.M.*, p. 32.

distinguish between particular sexual acts (which may or may not be procreative) and the sphere or realm of sexuality (which should be both unitive and procreative).

On this basis, AID, egg donation and IVF all separate these two ends of human sexuality in principle. They thus disrupt the very sphere or realm of sexuality: they are not simply isolated acts leading to procreation without love. Just as promiscuity outside marriage disrupts this sphere (but for opposite reasons), so do the biotechnological practices essential to active genetic control.

If this much is not immediately obvious in the context of AID, egg donation and embryo donation (which after all tend to be used in situations of deep care and compassion), Ramsey believed that it becomes so if cloning is envisaged as a possible future means of actively pursuing genetic control. Cloning, through removing the nucleus from a fertilised ovum and replacing it with a nucleus from an adult human (today termed 'nucleus substitution'), if it were ever possible, would have certain functional advantages over other methods of genetic control. Provided that donors of the replacement nuclei were chosen with sufficient care, the resulting babies should be freer from genetic defects. Indeed they should be freer from genetic defects than the progeny of sexual reproduction – which always contain a risk of the unknown. And the carrier of a serious recessive disorder could produce a clone without fear of the disorder becoming active. Whatever other functions might be suggested for cloning (providing spare parts, everlasting spouses, interesting scientific experiments, etc.), asexual reproduction would have specific advantages in the context of preventing further genetic deterioration resulting from modern medicine.

For Ramsey these were not advantages which outweigh the sheer immorality of human cloning. Arguing consequentially, Ramsey asked about the fate of the inevitable 'mishaps' that would result from attempts to renucleate fertilised ova. Using the obvious example of failed and partially successful experiments along the path to cloning frogs or mice, he pointed out that human nucleus substitution would inevitably result in many mishaps: 'in case a monstrosity – a subhuman or parahuman individual – results, shall the experiment simply be stopped and this artfully created human life killed?'.[8] Indeed, by envisaging such monstrous possibilities in current fiction and drama twenty years later, many today may share Ramsey's repugnance.

However, it was deontology, in the form of his theological commitments, which formed the heart of Ramsey's objections to human cloning. For him, 'the genetic proposal to clone a man, and the minority practice of artificial insemination from a non-husband donor, are borderlines that throw into bold relief *the nature of human parenthood* which both place under assault. If cloning men had no other consequence, this alone would be sufficient to fault it'.[9] In an even more extreme form than AID, human cloning separates the unitive and procreative ends of human sexuality. With obvious passion, he argued:

> 'To put radically asunder what nature and nature's God joined together in parenthood when he made love procreative, to disregard the foundation of the covenant of marriage and the covenant of parenthood in the reality that makes for a least minimally loving procreation, to attempt to soar so high above an eminently human parenthood, is inevitably to fall far below – into a vast technological alienation of man. Limitless dominion over procreation means the boundless servility of man-womanhood. The conquest of evolution by setting sexual love and procreation radically asunder entails depersonalisation in the extreme.'[10]

For Ramsey there was a sharp contrast between the bio-technologist's vision of human beings as limitless self-modifiers (the 'fabricated man' of the title) and the Jewish and Christian visions. It was the proper task of Christian ethics to challenge this particular secular world. Quite apart from the problem of properly understanding the multi-variables at stake in limitless self-modification, the biotechnologist's overall undertaking was held to display a questionable aspiration to Godhead. Ramsey's maxim was that 'men ought not to play God before they learn to be men, and after they have learned to be men they will not play God'.[11] He even accused some molecular biologists of 'messianic

[8] *F.M.*, p. 78.
[9] *F.M.*, p. 86–7.
[10] *F.M.*, p. 89.
[11] *F.M.*, p. 138.

positivism' and clearly believed that they had abrogated religious functions to themselves. And he concluded his book on a note of irony:

> 'With Brow Serene the Space Child will declare, as Augustine said of the Manichees, these men do not accept with good and simple faith that for one good and simple reason God created the world – because it is good.'[12]

3

In the twenty years since *Fabricated Man* was written a number of empirical changes have taken place. Passive genetic control has been greatly assisted by the routine availability of amniocentesis – a procedure in which amniotic fluid is withdrawn using a needle through the lower abdominal wall with the aim of screening for neural tube defects and for chromosomal abnormality. If direct action, in the form of induced abortion, is taken as a result of detecting some disorder, it is of necessity distressingly late (around 20 weeks). However, chorion villous sampling – a sometimes risky technique involving the removal of a small part of the fetal membrane – now offers the possibility of first trimester abortion. Fetoscopy, fetal blood sampling and ultrasound screening also can be used to detect a growing number of genetic disorders or serious abnormality of the fetus in early pregnancy.

Genetic counselling plays an increasingly important and complex role in modern medicine.[13] It has been estimated that in developed countries wholly or partially inherited disorders now account for perhaps a quarter of hospital admissions of children and are a major factor in half of childhood deaths.[14] Of course if genetic deterioration is unchecked these proportions will increase

[12] *F.M.*, p. 160.
[13] See A. Arnold and R. Mosely, 'Ethical Issues Arising from Medical Genetics', *Journal of Medical Ethics*, 1976, 2, 12–17; M. J. Seller, 'Ethical Aspects of Genetic Counselling', *Journal of Medical Ethics*, 1982, 8, 185–88; and R. West, 'Ethical Aspects of Genetic Disease and Genetic Counselling', *Journal of Medical Ethics*, 1988, 14, 194–7.
[14] West, 1988, cites A. E. H. Emery and D. L. Rimoin, 'Nature and Incidence of Genetic Disease', in A. E. H. Emery and D. L. Rimoin (eds.), *Principles and Practice of Medical Genetics*, Churchill Livingstone, Edinburgh, 1983, 1–3.

considerably in the future. Dr Richard West, having been a consultant to the St George's Hospital Genetic Counselling Clinic, illustrates some of the complexities of modern genetic counselling:

> 'Making a genetic diagnosis may have implications for some members of the extended family. For instance the sisters of a woman whose child has an X-linked disorder may also be carriers; a patient with a dominant disorder like Huntingdon's chorea may have first and second degree relatives who also carry the gene, and may pass it on; and in a family where consanguinity is common a recessive disorder may recur in other sibships. The doctor has a duty to other family members even if he has a special relationship with one family member.'[15]

This illustration also serves to highlight an additional ethical dilemma. The patient who insists upon medical confidentiality may pose a very real threat to present or future partners and especially to their children. The genetic counsellor who is attempting to take a holistic view may, like those counselling active HIV positive prostitutes, find a serious moral conflict here[16] (the final Chapter will return to this conflict).

Active genetic control has probably shown the most significant developments. AID was already a possibility when Ramsey wrote. Egg donation and embryo donation were only futuristic possibilities. The birth of the first child resulting from *in vitro* fertilisation in July 1978 radically changed this situation. A decade later IVF and now GIFT (gamete intra fallopian transfer) are used regularly, and pregnancies have resulted from frozen sperm and even embryos. And today AID is so common that every GP is likely to have encountered it directly – although for reasons of confidentiality, and in some cases its extra-medical application, it is difficult to be confident about its level of occurrence. Le Roy Walters expresses the present range of possibilities pithily when he writes: 'One implication of these new reproductive technologies is that a child can have up to three types of mothers (genetic, gestational, and social) and up to two

---

[15] West, 1988, p. 196.
[16] See Raanan Gillon, 'Genetic Counselling, Confidentiality, and the Medical Interests of Relatives', *Journal of Medical Ethics*, 1988, 14, 171–2.

types of fathers (genetic and social)'.[17] All of these techniques are predominantly used for the infertile. Yet they also have a major role in the control of genetic disorders.

It is also possible to foresee techniques which could be used for the control of sex-linked genetic disorders. Gender identification can already be achieved through the use of either high-resolution ultra-sound scan or amniocentesis. Late abortions of fetuses of the particular sex associated with a genetic disorder can then be offered to parents at severe risk. It is even possible in some cases to identify specific defective genes and thus to abort potential carriers as well. With the considerable research currently being done on attempting to map the genome (i.e. the total make-up of all the genes in a human cell) identification of defective genes should become increasingly accurate. Chorion villous sampling would again allow for first trimester abortions for those in these categories. IVF offers a non-abortive alternative if sex could be established in an embryo without damaging it. It might even be possible to separate male- and female-bearing sperm and then to use AID, GIFT or IVF to achieve a pregnancy without the risk of a specific sex-linked genetic disorder. Biochemical means might alternatively be discovered to make the woman more receptive to male- or female-bearing sperm – thus obviating the need for additional biotechnology.

In his discussion of cloning Ramsey focused upon what is now termed nucleus substitution. The Warnock Report instead reserves the term 'cloning' for the production of two or more genetically identical individuals through the division of the embryo at a very early stage of development. Such cloning could be spontaneous (as in identical twins) or induced. In this less threatening form the Warnock Report suggests a variation as a future possibility for genetic control:

> 'After *in vitro* fertilisation, the embryo would be allowed to develop until it was possible to remove one or more cells without putting at risk the subsequent development of the embryo. This technique is termed embryonic biopsy. The cells of the biopsy would be allowed to continue to develop while

[17] Le Roy Walters, 'Editor's Introduction to the Issue on Genetic and Reproductive Engineering', *The Journal of Medicine and Philosophy*, 10, 3, 1985, p. 209.

the rest of the embryo would be frozen. Once it was possible to determine from the biopsy whether the embryo was free from the abnormality for which it was being tested, a decision could be taken as to whether to thaw the frozen embryo and to transfer it to the mother's uterus.'[18]

Biochemical, viral or micro-surgical means of genetic control still remain mainly futuristic possibilities, although it is perhaps easier now to spot the directions that they might take. Methods are already being developed for micro-injecting foreign DNA into non-human embryos and for the insertion of DNA using retroviral vectors. The fabrication of viruses to act in specific and controllable ways is being increasingly established. Specific viruses manufactured to replace defective genes would offer a very obvious way of preventing genetic deterioration. Again, micro-surgery, relying upon IVF, successfully isolating and removing defective genes at a very early stage of embryonic development may not be entirely fanciful. Advances made initially for agricultural purposes might one day pave the way for micro-surgical means of genetic control. And biochemistry, as already noted, may play a part in eliminating sex-linked genetic defects. Biochemical preventive measures may also become more common. For example, it now seems probable that the incidence of spina bifida is lowered in high-risk families where women take vitamin and mineral supplements before conception.

For the most part the biotechnological developments relevant to genetic control over the last twenty years are refinements of techniques already envisaged by Ramsey. For this reason his ethical and theological considerations are as relevant today as they were when he wrote *Fabricated Man*.[19] The more fanciful elements – such as human nucleus substitution, trans-species fertilisation involving human genetic material, human partheno-genesis or ectogenesis – remain as fanciful as ever. Since he

[18] *Report of the Committee of Inquiry into Human Fertilisation and Embryology*, Chairman, Dame Mary Warnock, HMSO, London, July 1984, 12.12.

[19] See further, L. Walters, *Human in Vitro Fertilisation: A Review of the Ethical Literature*, Hastings Centre Report, New York, 1979; G. R. Dunstan, 'In Vitro Fertilisation: The Ethical Debate', in S. Fishel and E. M. Symonds, *In Vitro Fertilisation; Past, Present and Future*, IRL Press, Oxford and Washington DC, 1986, 171–85.

rightly rejected thin-end-of-wedge arguments, it will not do to assess the moral legitimacy of less fanciful techniques in the light of these extremes. 'Cloning', for example, in the sense given to it in the Warnock Report should not be assessed in the light of 'cloning' envisaged and properly condemned by Ramsey.

There is a general ethical warning running throughout *Fabricated Man* against manufacturing a genetic future for humanity whose variables we cannot control. For example, after discussing the futuristic possibility of biochemical and microsurgical genetic control Ramsey warned that 'the science of genetics (and medical practice based on it) would be obliged both to be fully informed of the facts of doing more good than harm by eliminating the genetic defect in question'.[20] And at several points he expressed the modern despair about our genetic future in epigrammatic terms:

> 'Because those who come after us may not be like us, or because those like us may not come after us, or because after a time there may be none to come after us, mankind must now set to work to ensure that those who come after us will be more and more unlike us.'[21]

Twenty years later similar prudential warnings are regularly voiced in the context of agricultural biotechnology.[22] For instance, as mentioned in the Introduction, genetically adapted grain seeds, whilst effecting the highly beneficial 'green revolution' in parts of the Developing World, have also raised very real concern about the consequent diminishment of the genetic constituents of natural seed stock. Over-reliance upon genetically adapted seeds makes farmers vulnerable to the possibility of diseases that the genetic material of non-adapted seeds might have been able to resist. Scientists, the very architects of the new genetic seeds, indirectly cause the gradual disappearance of a primary natural resource from which they might in the future

[20] *F.M.*, pp. 44–5.
[21] *F.M.*, pp. 159–60.
[22] See A. Bull, G. Holt and M. D. Lilly, *Biotechnology: International Trends and Perspectives*, Organisation for Economic Co-operation and Development, Paris 1982; E. Yoxen, *The Gene Business: Who Should Control Biotechnology?*, Pan and Channel Four, London, 1983; S. Yanchinski, *Setting Genes to Work: The Industrial Era of Biotechnology*, Viking/Penguin, Middlesex, 1985.

construct further genetic seeds capable of resisting presently unforeseen blights. Ironically, it also makes farmers more vulnerable to, and dependent upon, the international conglomerates that produce the adapted seeds, since these conglomerates increasingly seek to patent their products even within the Developing World. If they are successful in this patenting, already impoverished farmers will be required to buy their seeds anew each year. It will become illegal for them simply to replant a portion of their own yield. Thus their genetically adapted seeds would be vulnerable to unforeseen disease and they themselves would be vulnerable to the avarice of the international conglomerates.

Every scientific advance may contain the risk of unforeseen future consequences – although some of Ramsey's fears about fetal abnormalities arising from IVF now appear unfounded.[23] It will be no surprise to those who have long been used to the phenomenon of iatrogenesis, to discover that advances in medicine sometimes bring in their wake fresh medical problems. This is especially the case when we become over-dependent upon medication (social iatrogenesis). In this respect biochemical, viral and micro-surgical developments in genetic control would be little different from other aspects of medicine. If human genetic intervention were ever to become as ubiquitous as agricultural genetic intervention (and that is a very large 'if'), then there surely would be grounds for Ramsey's pessimism. Yet at present prudence and vigilance might be more appropriate moral responses.

Further, given that research into genetic intervention in the interests of preventing genetic defects is likely to receive overwhelming public support, Christian ethicists surely cannot reasonably expect it to be halted simply because its future consequences are unknown. As John Fletcher argues, 'to ban gene experiments that may help today's children in the name of protection from uncertain dangers of future uses of gene technology would be to act irrationally *and* unfairly'.[24]

[23] See P. Singer and D. Wells, *The Reproductive Revolution: New Ways of Making Babies*, OUP, Oxford, New York and Melbourne, 1984, pp. 46–9.
[24] J. C. Fletcher, 'Ethical Issues in and Beyond Prospective Clinical Trials of Human Gene Therapy', *The Journal of Medicine and Philosophy*, 10, 3, 1985, p. 301.

Nevertheless, Christian ethicists in this secular world of biotechnology can properly seek to foster the moral responsibility already present amongst many scientists. It *is* the latter's duty to keep in mind the present and, where discernible, future, welfare of those with genetic disorders – and indeed the actual and potential risks of their work to the community at large.

Ramsey's fiercest moral strictures fell on the second group of techniques to prevent genetic deterioration. It is on these then that I must concentrate – although, as noted, the third group also tends to use IVF today. The very techniques that Ramsey most castigated have now become widely accepted medical practice. Specifically, the techniques involving a separation of unitive and procreative ends in human sexuality (AID, egg donation, GIFT and IVF) – together with selective abortion following amniocentesis – today constitute the principle medical means of preventing genetic defects. His counsel of vocational childlessness for those at risk of some grave genetic defect, or indeed for those who are simply infertile, is largely unheeded. Instead, considerable medical resources are committed to practising and furthering the techniques he rejected.

It is by no means clear that Ramsey's position was wholly consistent. His stress upon the distinction between sexual acts and sexual realms may have saved him from some of the most obvious criticisms facing his injunctions against separating the unitive and procreative ends of sexuality. Although even *Humanae Vitae* specifically mentioned that 'new life is not the result of each and every act of sexual intercourse'.[25] Yet it did not spare him from the question of why single incidences of AID should not themselves be regarded as 'acts'. Why do they disturb the realm of human sexuality? Interestingly, AIH and certain uses of IVF are today accepted by some Catholic moral theologians such as Jack Mahoney.[26] Of course, it is possible to envisage a *Brave New World* in which the two ends of sexuality are wholly separated, with ectogenesis becoming the norm, but I suspect that this is more a novelist's dream than a serious possibility. And in the limited context of preventing genetic deterioration it is surely pure fantasy.

[25] *Humanae Vitae*, para. 11.
[26] J. Mahoney, SJ, *Bioethics and Belief*, Sheed and Ward, London, 1984.

Ramsey's position is also questionable on theological grounds. He (and *Humanae Vitae*) had a strangely static understanding of Creation. God created the world in this way, and in this way it must remain. Unfortunately it is this understanding which has underpinned many past theological attempts to halt scientific developments and perhaps science itself. A more dynamic understanding of Creation might suggest instead that humans are, in some sense, co-creators or co-workers with God. The scientist/theologian A. R. Peacocke even suggests boldly that humans may be 'co-explorers' with God, exploring through science and technology 'with God the creative possibilities within the universe God has brought into being'.[27] And Ian Barbour, as seen in the previous Chapter, has consistently used Process theology to depict God in dynamic terms. If all of that is thought to confuse creature with Creator,[28] then at least it can be argued that God uses human developments to further divine intentions. If the prevention of genetic deterioration is itself part of the divine intention, then those engaged in genetic research may on this understanding be seen as a part of God's work in the world.

Such theological understandings may actually encourage scientists to continue to act as responsible human beings and to remember the proper ends for which they work.[29] At the same time they may discourage Christian ethicists from imagining that, God has made human sexuality in this or that way, and so it should invariably and in all circumstances remain.

5

The key to my own ethical position in matters of human sexuality is one of responsibility. I have already expressed strong reservations in Chapter 1 about that aspect of the Natural Law

[27] A. R. Peacocke, *Creation and the World of Science*, Clarendon Press, Oxford, 1979, p. 306.

[28] See J. M. Gustafson, *Ethics from a Theocentric Perspective*, Vol. I, *Theology and Ethics*, University of Chicago Press, Chicago, 1981; D. Gareth Jones, *Brave New People: Ethical Issues at the Commencement of Life*, Inter-Varsity Press, Leicester, 1984.

[29] See R. S. Cole-Turner, 'Is Genetic Engineering Co-Creation?', *Theology Today*, 1987, 338–49.

tradition, mediated so strongly through Aquinas, whereby 'every emission of semen, in such a way that generation cannot follow, is contrary to the good for man'.[30] Nor am I very convinced by its modern equivalent that 'every emission of semen outside the vagina, in such a way that generation does follow, is contrary to the good for man'. But I am thoroughly convinced by Aquinas' insistence that the generation of a child carries responsibilities for both of the parents of that child. From this perspective, it could be that the loving parents of a child born as a result of AID, egg donation, GIFT or IVF, specifically to avoid the risk of a grave genetic defect, are acting more responsibly than conventional couples who divorce when their children most need them. In the context of current statistics about divorce, single parent families and child abuse (factors which may not be unrelated), it is arguable that our society has much to learn about responsible parenthood. In contrast, those couples who are infertile but desperate to have children, or those couples who are fertile but actively seek to avoid a known genetic risk, may have much to teach the rest of us about responsible parenthood.

In this new and potentially dangerous world of active genetic control it is proper for the Christian ethicist to remain vigilant. Paul Ramsey's *Fabricated Man* remains a model of vigilance and courage. But it also remains a very partial model of doing Christian ethics in secular worlds. It might still serve to encourage genetic scientists to act responsibly in our short-term and long-term interests. Twenty years later prudence and vigilance are still required. Yet its very vehemence and denunciations severely distorted the ethical dilemmas it sought to uncover. It treated scientists like moral infants and advanced nightmares which can now be seen indeed to have been dreams. In short, it challenged before it listened.

Christian ethicists in this bewildering secular world might be better advised to follow the Ian Ramsey approach instead. Strident denunciation is not an adequate substitute for working patiently alongside creative scientists, uncertain themselves about the ethical consequences and opportunities of their work.

---

[30] *Summa Contra Gentiles*, 3.2.122.

Part 3

Society

6

The Moral Function of Religion

At several points in this book I have given warning that I will
return at length to what might be described as the moral function
of religion. Christian ethicists in secular worlds sometimes find
themselves immersed in the minutiae of biotechnology, of multi-
layered nuclear strategies, of interacting ecological factors, or of
other complex political or technological issues. At other times we
are more concerned with the general underlying values that may
shape society and of which most people in society are largely
oblivious. Micro-complexities and macro-ambiguities are both
part of doing Christian ethics in secular worlds. In this chapter I
will focus on the latter.

The belief that the primary social function of religion lies in
the area of corporate morality is well entrenched in Western
thought. It certainly predates the Humean revolution in philosophy and has survived it in popular thought, and especially in the
social sciences, remarkably intact. Even if (despite MacIntyre) it
is thought that moral philosophy as an intellectual discipline
informing intellectuals is logically distinct from any religious
basis, moral behaviour and moral presuppositions in society
more generally, are still frequently believed to derive from
religious positions. There even seems to be evidence in a number
of disciplines that a belief in the moral function of religion is
gaining some surprising supporters.

This chapter sets out to do three things. Firstly, it will sketch
some of the forms this belief is currently taking both in the
sociology of religion and in comparative religious ethics.
Secondly, it will outline some of the main difficulties that
confront claims about the moral function of religion. And

thirdly, it will suggest a specific way in which a more limited version of this claim might be defended.

I

The central issue here has relevance far beyond the narrow technical literature of these two disciplines. In many respects it lies at the very heart of many attempts to do Christian ethics in secular worlds. The celebrated debate between Lord Devlin and H. L. A. Hart[1] in the 1960s on the relation between law, morality and religion was as much about this as about anything else.

In his critical commentary on this debate, Basil Mitchell entitled one of his chapters 'In What Sense is a Shared Morality Essential for Society?'. As this was the 1960s the concept of 'a shared morality' was largely discussed in the debate in terms of sexual morality. And in response to his own question Mitchell argued (albeit in terms that appear distinctly less plausible today):

> 'No society is content to allow relations between the sexes to be entirely a matter of individual preference. And if a society chooses to insist on a single pattern, it is difficult to believe that it is *eo ipso* guilty of unwarrantable interference with the freedom of its members. Thus it seems to me that Devlin is right in holding that the law may take the line that monogamy as an institution is essential to our society and be justified in taking it.'[2]

Mitchell was fully aware that in this respect society might change over time (and evidently has changed much faster than he anticipated) and that other societies might decide differently. Nevertheless, speaking specifically of Britain in the 1960s, he was convinced that it 'is beyond dispute that the traditional institutions of our society have been deeply influenced by Christianity, so that any movement to reform them must take account of the Christian ideas underlying them'.[3]

Furthermore, in the current debate within theology between

[1] See H. L. A. Hart, *Law, Liberty and Morality*, OUP 1963, and Patrick Devlin, *The Enforcement of Morals*, OUP 1965.
[2] Basil Mitchell, *Law, Morality, and Religion*, OUP 1967, p. 30.
[3] ibid., p. 126.

Don Cupitt and others, as was suggested in Chapter 1, one of the central features is the issue of whether or not religion can be identified with morality. Arguably for Cupitt Christianity is more a moral code or a guide to living than a transcendent perspective. For him it seems to be the moral function of Christianity which is its primary feature.

Cupitt's position has changed very considerably over the last twenty years and doubtless will change again. In *Crisis of Moral Authority* in the early 1970s he criticised traditional ascetical disciplines as 'morally objectionable at just the points where it is not true to Christian theism. Too much in it was a lapse from Christian theism back to earlier patterns of religious thought'.[4] However, in the next decade it was theism which he rejected and a form of moral asceticism which he proposed instead. So, thirteen years later in *Only Human* he concluded:

> 'One thing remained: even if true religion could no longer be defined in terms of a true objective content believed, there was still surely a difference in character between a truly religious person and a superstitious person. For a truly religious person is distinguished by a particular kind of purity of heart or integrity of will, a quality of unconditional dedication of his whole life, a sense of his vocation and of his life as a pilgrimage, which is unmistakable ... The objects of faith, such as God, are seen as guiding spiritual ideals that we live by, and not as beings ... Religious activity has now to be undertaken just for its own sake, as an autonomous and practical response to the coolly perceived truth of the human condition. This is true religion: all else is superstition.'[5]

In contrast, John Habgood in his influential book *Church and Nation in a Secular Age* is emphatic that morality and theology should not be treated interchangeably:

> 'Christianity is not just about values. Nor is its primary purpose to secure social stability, though this may in practice emerge as one of its useful functions. A faith reduced to this

[4] Don Cupitt, *Crisis of Moral Authority: The Dethronement of Christianity*, Lutterworth 1972, p. 47.
[5] Don Cupitt, *Only Human*, SCM Press 1985, pp. 201–2.

role, however, would have become as secularised as the society in which it is set.'[6]

Yet, having stated that, the rest of his book argues strongly that religion in general, and the Church of England in particular, does have a very specific and crucial moral/social function. Indeed, Habgood contends that when a pluralist society comes under threat it is religious values that may protect it more adequately than values derived from other sources:

> 'Logically the conclusion seems inescapable that a fully pluralist state, which was that and nothing more, could only survive by drawing from time to time on values outside its own commitment to pluralism.'[7]

2

The notion that the primary social function of religion is to integrate society frequently recurs in the sociology of religion. Through the French intellectual tradition, in particular, it has often been assumed that religion is a key factor in integrating traditional societies, that religion is now in terminal demise, and that this poses fundamental problems for the future well-being and integration of modern society. Given these assumptions, it is hardly surprising that French intellectuals have, at various times, sought functional substitutes for supernatural religion by means of which the masses might assimilate values deemed essential for social integration.

An alternative to this Comtian optimism has been the social pessimism apparent from Durkheim to Sartre; supernatural religion is no longer socially credible and people must survive as best they can without it. Despite the well-known methodological weaknesses[8] of *The Elementary Forms of the Religious Life*, its central convictions about the social function of religion – *all* religion – persist strongly in modern sociology of religion.

[6] John Habgood, *Church and Nation in a Secular Age*, Darton, Longman and Todd 1983, p. 49.

[7] ibid., p. 34.

[8] See W. S. F. Pickering, *Durkheim on Religion*, Routledge and Kegan Paul 1975, and Durkheim's *Sociology of Religion*, Routledge and Kegan Paul 1984.

This is very evident in Bryan Wilson's various, and highly influential, writings on secularisation. So, in *Religion in Sociological Perspective*, he views secularisation as a shift from a religiously based community, or *Gemeinschaft*, to a rationally and technologically based associational society, or *Gesellschaft*, bringing individual benefits but also social dangers:

'Religion, by which I mean the invocation of the supernatural, was the ideology of community. In every context of traditional life, we may see religious symbolism and religious performances used to celebrate and legitimate local life. There were religious procedures to protect the local settlement; there were supernatural agents to whom the family or the clan and its members could relate; by reference to religion men were reassured of their power, secured in their status, justified in their wealth, or consoled for their poverty. Religion could give the best guarantees of fertility for mankind and the abundance of the means of sustenance. It provided the means for according public recognition and identification to the young; and for coping with bereavement. Its points of reference were to things local (some of which were, of course, also things universal). All of these one-time functions of religion have declined in significance as human involvements have ceased to be communal. Industrial society needs no local gods, or local saints; no local nostrums, remedies, or points of reference. The means of sustenance are not local.'[9]

Like Durkheim, Wilson frequently supposes a strong connection between religion and the moral order in traditional society. For him, 'the traditional patterns of order were sustained by what, at their best, were shared intimations and apprehensions of the supernatural. The moral order was, ultimately, order derived from intimations (of whatever specific kind) of a super-empirical sphere'. But today the situation is quite different: 'in the advanced societal system, the supernatural plays no part in the perceived, experienced, and instituted order. The environment is hostile to the super-empirical: it relies on rational, humanly conceived, planned procedures, in the operation of which there is no room for extra-empirical propositions, or random inspira-

[9] Bryan Wilson, *Religion in Sociological Perspective*, OUP 1982, p. 59.

tional intuitions'.[10] Thus, 'community has been severely weakened, and even intimate relationships are now invaded by our dependence on technical devices (for example, in such matters as birth control), and by the constraints of rationally ordered required performances'.[11]

It is apparent from this that Wilson is now more pessimistic about the future of society than Durkheim was earlier in the century: 'Durkheim saw the problem of advanced society – that it would need goodwill, disinterested affection if it were to work, but he did not adequately realise the extent to which the rational premises of the new order would destroy this attribute of the moral community.'[12]

It is precisely the need for such altruistic attributes as 'goodwill' and 'disinterested affection' in society that prompts Ronald Green to argue that religion is basically a form (indeed, an essential form) of moral reasoning. Writing from the perspective of comparative religious ethics, rather than from that of the sociology of religion, he presents an unusual and powerfully argued case for believing that religion is indeed an essential element in social integration.

In his book, *Religious Reason: The Rational and Moral Basis of Religious Belief*, Green maintains that religious belief is basically a rational form of activity concerned primarily with human attempts to control natural and social environments. It is a form of activity closely associated with moral reasoning. A difference between the two is that religious reasoning is able to complete tasks which are unresolved in pure moral reasoning. Further, 'by identifying the rational program underlying the development of several important historical traditions of belief, I have tried to suggest the essential rationality and intelligibility of these traditions'.[13] Thus, from a position of relative detachment from any specific religious tradition, Green believes that he can 'penetrate and lay bare the basic and universal structure of reason which underlies religion – which I call "pure religious reason"'.[14]

[10] ibid., p. 162.
[11] ibid., p. 163.
[12] ibid., p. 166.
[13] Ronald M. Green, *Religious Reason*, OUP 1978, p. 247 (see also Chapter 1 of his *Religion and Moral Reason*, OUP 1988).
[14] ibid., p. 7.

Following Kant, Green believes that the need for morality can be rationally demonstrated. He believes that objective moral rules or imperatives can be set out – rules that can be universalised and thus apply to all mankind. But, again like Kant, he believes that pure moral reasoning is unable to answer certain crucial questions about the individual moral agent. Notably, it can give no satisfactory answer to questions about why any particular moral agent should always act morally or about whether anyone is capable of always acting morally. It is religious reasoning alone, which can give a satisfactory answer to these two questions.

The first question concerns the difficulty of convincing particular individuals that it is rational for them to act morally when it does not appear to be in their particular interests to do so. Thus, if 'happiness' is thought to be an important end of morality, particular situations which will not necessarily lead to happiness and yet which are morally right for mankind as a whole, will create problems for individuals. At issue here is a conflict between self and society (a problem that will be highlighted in the final chapter on the ethics of AIDS and social control). An individual may be persuaded of the need for moral rules in society, yet that same individual still has to be persuaded that it is his or her duty personally to follow these rules even when they conflict with personal interests. Thus, 'rational individuals commonly find it very hard to uphold standards that they concede to be morally valid. Indeed, it is a partial indication of how difficult it is to answer the question 'Why should I be moral?' that sexual infidelity or graft sometimes attract the best of persons'.[15]

Thus, for Green an impasse is reached: 'though reason can provide a general justification of moral obedience, it cannot justify such obedience to every individual in every case. But this amounts to saying that reason cannot furnish a complete justification of moral obedience at all. So long as every rational individual knows that in some cases, at least, it will be in some respect irrational to be moral, he cannot give his unwavering and absolute support to the moral rules, although that is just what

[15] ibid., pp. 43–4.

morality demands'.[16] Like Kant, Green believes that religion resolves this dilemma, although, unlike Kant, he attempts to express this in language which is religious but not necessarily theistic (he is concerned to formulate his answer so that it relates to Eastern, non-theistic forms of religion):

> '"How, in situations where my happiness is jeopardised by moral obedience, can I act rationally at all?". The answer . . . is that I can act rationally if I obey the moral rules and at the same time hold certain specific beliefs not supported by experience. These beliefs – they can be called, for convenience, metaphysical or religious – have the effect of persuading me that the course of moral obedience may not be imprudent at all, and they render that course an acceptable alternative . . . impartial reason has been compelled, in order to render its whole enterprise coherent, to postulate certain necessary supra-empirical beliefs. It is true that at this point these beliefs are only skeletal in character and have very little in common with the kind of religious propositions with which we are familiar. Specifically, these beliefs required by reason include a belief in the possibly real existence of a form of causality, a causal agency, that is both perfectly moral and in some way supreme over nature.'[17]

The second question concerns the difficulty of believing that anyone is actually capable of being continuously moral. Yet the logic of morality itself requires that all should be perfect. Moral perfection, then, seems to be required by moral reasoning, but seems empirically unattainable. The moral agent can become paralysed by this dilemma, since he or she is apparently required to do something which, because of the frailties of human nature, simply cannot be done. Again, Kant was acutely aware of this moral dilemma, yet Green wishes to express his religious solution in a somewhat broader, and less specifically theistic, manner:

> 'At just this point the "supreme" component in the idea of a supreme and perfectly moral causal agency can perform a decisive role, for in its supremacy that agency may be thought of not only as the ground of nature but somehow of all reality

[16] ibid., p. 58.
[17] ibid., p. 73.

as well. That suggests that we, with our morality and our moral judgements, are in some way a product of its activity. All of our judgements, in other words, including our most pressing moral judgements, may be thought of as not necessarily absolute but as one expression, possibly only a partial expression, of the supreme and perfect moral agency from which they derive.'[18]

3

However attractive is the notion that the primary function of religion is to integrate society by supplying it with a moral basis, it faces a fundamental problem. This applies equally to sociologists such as Wilson as it does to ethicists such as Green. For the notion to be viable it must be possible to identify 'religion' and to differentiate it from 'non-religion'. Clearly statements about 'religion as a whole' and 'the social function of religion' soon become vacuous if this is not possible.

Durkheim himself was well aware that this is so: 'it is necessary to begin by defining what is meant by a religion; for without this, we would run the risk of giving the name to a system of ideas and practices which has nothing at all religious about it, or else of leaving to one side many religious facts, without perceiving their true nature'.[19] He then proceeded to take his contemporaries to task at length for what he regarded as their false conceptions of what constitutes 'religion'. Durkheim believed both that he could define 'religion' and that he could identify it in its most 'primitive' and simplest form. In the circumstances it is not so surprising that he then felt that he could reach overarching conclusions about the social function of religion as a whole.

Most present-day sociologists are far more cautious than Durkheim was about producing a formal definition of religion (Wilson's notion[20] of religion as 'the invocation of the supernatural' is clearly not a formal definition) and few indeed would support his evolutionary assumptions about 'primitive' religion,

---

[18] ibid., p. 104.
[19] Emile Durkheim, *The Elementary Forms of the Religious Life*, Allen and Unwin 1976 ed., p. 23.
[20] op. cit.

let alone his actual identification of this with the Arunta of Australia. Nonetheless they still talk about 'religion' and speculate about its social function or about its social demise. Frequently they do so on the basis of a claim that whereas it may not be possible to produce a single, formal definition of 'religion', it is nonetheless possible to identify particular religions. They point out that there are many social phenomena which elude formal definition but which can still be identified and differentiated from other phenomena.

Often they proceed to use Wittgenstein's notion of family resemblances to show how it is possible to identify a member of a particular family from shared family characteristics, even though there will be no single characteristic which every member of the family possesses. On this analogy, it is thought possible to compile a set of characteristics which typically belong to religions (e.g. supernatural beliefs, ritual practices, numinous experiences, etc.), but which may not all be present in every religion (e.g. the relative lack of supernatural beliefs in Theravada Buddhism).

Unfortunately, although widely adopted, this analogy has very obvious flaws. At the simplest level it is possible to ask how many characteristics something must have to be classified as a religion. If analysts can agree upon (say) eight defining characteristics and are also agreed that particular religions may not have all eight, just how many must they have to be identified as religions? This is no verbal wrangle since it affects one's understanding of the social function of religion very profoundly if one is allowed to include such phenomena as magic, belief in ghosts, strongly held ideologies, or even Communism, under the label 'religion'.

Of even greater concern is the problem that the analogy of family resemblances only works if one can *already* identify who belongs to the family. Then, and only then, can one compile the necessary list of defining characteristics. Yet, in the case of religion, it is the membership of the family which is itself in dispute.

I believe that this problem should worry sociologists and religionists more than it apparently does. For certain purposes it may not matter too much that 'religion' cannot be satisfactorily defined or even identified. There are sufficient characteristics in common between, for example, Islam and Christianity for them to be usefully compared. But if more general claims are to be made about 'religion as a whole', whether in terms of its overall social function or in terms of a thoroughgoing secularisation thesis, it certainly does matter. I suspect that such claims only have plausibility in the West because the Western understanding of religion has already been moulded by Judaeo–Christian concepts. Within this context Wilson's depiction of religion as 'the invocation of the supernatural' or Green's thoroughly cognitive (and Kantian/Protestant) concept of religion might appear plausible. However, within a non-Western context, dependent upon very different plausibility structures, such depictions may not appear so convincing.

Indeed, those concerned with the academic study of 'religions' may have to learn that their task and the way they achieve this task are more culturally specific than once they imagined. Durkheim's overall theories about the social function of religion may still be interesting, but the way he established them is now so thoroughly discredited, that they really cannot be adopted without considerable reservations. Certainly overarching claims, like those in Bruce Reed's *The Dynamics of Religion*,[21] should be avoided.

This general point has been made forcefully in Stanley Jeyaraja Tambiah's *Magic, Science, Religion, and the Scope of Rationality*.[22] Tambiah is a social anthropologist who has read widely in social theory, philosophy and the history of science. Although educated and now teaching in the West (he is currently a professor at Harvard) he comes from and was first educated in Sri Lanka. He knows Western scholarship intimately but is also far more aware than most Western scholars of the cultural limitations from which it emanates. For him even science derives from culturally specific traditions.

A central theme of Tambiah's book is that debates about the nature of religion and magic in and beyond social anthropology owe more than a little to Western culture. He argues that this is

[21] SPCK 1978.
[22] Stanley Jeyaraja Tambiah, *Magic, Science, Religion, and the Scope of Rationality*, CUP 1990.

most obvious in Tylor's classic definition of religion as belief in spiritual beings – an eminently Protestant definition – but it is also apparent in many attempts to distinguish between religion and magic and then to oppose them separately or together to science. Frazer's work is also discussed in these terms – with fascinating notes by Wittgenstein on what he clearly regarded as Frazer's condescending notion of 'primitive' beliefs – together with the work of Malinowski and Levy-Bruhl.

After a lengthy discussion of rationality, relativism and modern science, Tambiah argues that Western thought becomes particularly dangerous when it transports the universal rationality of scientific causality into such areas as morality, economics and politics and then uses the whole as a yardstick for measuring, understanding and evaluating other cultures and civilisations. Not only does this distort other cultures (as some of the classic anthropologists did), but it also ignores the moral and political problems that science itself faces in the modern world. Indeed, it is with a moral argument that he concludes this fascinating study:

> 'Coming from a Third World country, how can I not appreciate how applied science has helped to curtail malaria, eradicate smallpox, reduce infant mortality, enable double cropping and the green revolution? But neither can I at the same time be unaware of or insensitive to the fact that these same benefits have taken their toll of cultural and social costs and unanticipated dislocating effects? Provided we do not reify science, and provided we are mindful that science can be used in the service of different ends, and that we who construct it have also the responsibility to regulate its use, science will unquestionably be deemed as indispensable to the human quest for freedom, creativity, prosperity and peace.'[23]

If the study of 'religions' should become more culturally specific, it is appropriate that the study of the social function of Christianity itself should be specific to particular cultures and social contexts. Thus to claim a social function for the Church of England is not to assume that British society cannot survive without religiously derived values. There is enough evidence from totalitarian states to suggest that politically engineered values can be imposed upon societies and serve to integrate those

[23] ibid., p. 154.

societies. For the theologian or ethicist mere social integration cannot be regarded as a sufficient criterion of the acceptability of a particular organisation or movement. Wars of conquest doubtless integrate both victors and victims, but they are not thereby morally or theologically justifiable. Moral values, and with them a moral and social order, can be evoked through deceit, tyranny or social manipulation, as well as through long-established religious traditions.

4

Nonetheless, it is possible that the moral and social order in British society is still deeply embedded in the Judaeo–Christian tradition. Without denying some of the tendencies that Wilson believes typify *Gesellschaft* society, it is possible to identify certain features of British society which are still apparently controlled by key values, themselves derived from a religious heritage. He admits himself that 'the comparison that I have made between community and society has been deliberately overdrawn'.[24] On this theory, values have become transposed from their Judaeo–Christian setting and are embedded, largely unrecognised, in a modern secular setting.

Using such a transposition thesis, I argued elsewhere[25] that Britain may not be as secularised as at first it might appear. It was, after all, Paul Halmos[26] who first suggested that *agape* was implicit within effective counselling, even though secular counsellors themselves usually disguise and deny it. Notions of care for those in need, of confidentiality, private honesty and personal responsibility, are now, in some respects, built into the structures of British society. Of course, they could change and Habgood's warning of a secular pluralist society under stress is important. But values may also be remarkably durable and may, as argued earlier, survive outside their original context rather longer than is sometimes imagined.

There is an obvious danger in this argument. It appears to

[24] op. cit., p. 163.
[25] See my *Prophecy and Praxis*, Marshall, Morgan and Scott 1981, and *Beyond Decline*, SCM Press 1988.
[26] Paul Halmos, *The Faith of the Counsellors*, Constable 1965.

ignore a growing critique within the sociology of religion of Durkheim's claims, or even those advanced half a century later by Talcott Parsons, about the social function of religion. If once it was widely assumed that religion binds societies together, it is more usual to find the assertion in recent writings in the sociology of religion that religions, especially in the modern world, tend rather to have thoroughly divisive and fragmentary social functions.

Bryan Turner's *Religion and Social Theory: a Materialist Perspective* is one of the most challenging books to propose this thesis. Turner argues strongly against the notion that religion 'can act as the social cement of modern society in the same way that it supposedly bound traditional societies together'. Far from binding society together, he maintains that:

> 'The empirical evidence points to significant religious differ-
> ences between social classes in terms of religious affiliation,
> style and practice . . . Societies are held together not simply or
> even primarily by common beliefs and ritual practices, but by a
> multitude of "material" factors – force, economic coercion,
> economic dependency, legal compulsion, economic scarcity,
> habituation and the exigencies of everyday life.'[27]

He is highly critical, for instance, of Bellah's notion of civil religion (discussed earlier in Chapter 2), presenting instead a materialist perspective on religion. He insists that this perspective is not reductionist, as so much Marxist analysis of religion has been in the past, but is rather a perspective which 'locates religion at the centre of social production and reproduction'.[28] Complaining (with some justice) that the concerns of sociologists of religion have latterly been too narrow, he seeks to raise fresh questions about how religion is related to the physical/material realms of politics, economics, property and sexuality.

It is an ambitious task, so perhaps it is not surprising that Turner makes many sweeping generalisations about these complex relationships over time and space. Part of his perspective is drawn from Engels and he takes examples, not just from Christianity, but from Judaism and Islam as well. In part his is a

[27] Bryan Turner, *Religion and Social Theory*, Heinemann 1983, p. 61.
[28] ibid., p. 2.

debunking task – reducing exaggerated claims about the social significance of religion in times past – but in part he also shares the epiphenominalist views of Bryan Wilson about the present-day social function of religion.

So, he argues that in feudal society, 'religion provided the symbolic medium by which the dominant class conceptualised its political relationships. The integration of feudal societies was *aided* by a common religious system, but this was not a *necessary* requirement'.[29] Within this society and in the early stages of capitalism the control of property inheritance was crucial and for this to be achieved it was important, again with the support of religion, to control female sexual activity. But, he maintains, these forms of support are no longer necessary to, or part of, late capitalist society. Such a society 'can "tolerate" extensive sexual, political and social deviance'.[30] Today, in sharp contrast to the Mitchell thesis of the 1960s, Turner argues that Western religion is a privatised phenomenon and that sexual behaviour is simply a matter of personal preference without major socio-political implications.

It is evident from this that Turner *is* an epiphenominalist and pays very little attention to the sort of modified claims already suggested, to the effect that Christian values may still inform British society. To support this last position it is not essential to claim that religious values are a necessary requirement for British society. Rather it need only be claimed that there is evidence in such institutions as the welfare state, concepts of justice and requirements for social care in contemporary Britain, to suggest that Christian values may still play an important (even if often invisible) role in an apparently secular society. On such a theory, these values affect the qualitative, although not necessarily the physical, survival of society. It is precisely these sort of modified claims that characterise Habgood's work. But Turner does not appear to consider such possibilities.

A rather different analysis is presented in James Beckford's recent book *Religion and Advanced Industrial Society*.[31] The

[29] ibid., p. 197.
[30] ibid., p. 198.
[31] James A. Beckford, *Religion and Advanced Industrial Society*, Unwin Hyman 1989.

central contention of this original book is that the sociology of
religion as a discipline has been too slow to realise that the nature
of industrial society has radically changed. The seminal works in
the discipline, by sociologists such as Weber and Durkheim,
were written in the context of a late nineteenth-century industrial
society. The advanced industrial society (or even post-industrial
society) of the late twentieth century is now so different that the
framework set by these classic studies is no longer appropriate if
we are to understand the complex roles that religion play today.
Yet, Beckford maintains, sociologists of religion have been too
slow to realise this, and have stuck to discussions about such
issues as 'secularisation' or 'church-sect typology' which no
longer fully fit this new situation.

In the early part of the book Beckford takes the reader through
the familiar territory of the seminal sociologists of religion, albeit
expounding his underlying thesis that their analyses no longer
fit advanced industrial society. He then examines American
attempts in the mid-twentieth century to understand the
function of religion. Talcott Parsons is again the dominant figure
here. Beckford establishes particularly clear and interesting
connections between his work and that of sociologists such as
Robert Bellah. In the light of the continuing influence of the
latter in the widely discussed *Habits of the Heart* noted in
Chapters 1 and 2, Beckford's criticisms are particularly pertinent.
In advanced industrial society, he believes, notions of shared
social values, still sought by Bellah, are anachronistic In the final
part of the book he argues that Marxist and semi-Marxist
sociologists, such as Habermas, Offe and Touraine, have insights
to offer sociologists of religion, precisely because they do take
advanced industrial society into account.

Beckford's judicious concluding paragraph is worth quoting in
full:

> 'From a sociological point of view, it is nowadays better to
> conceptualise religion as a cultural resource or form than as a
> social institution. As such, it is characterised by a greater
> degree of flexibility and unpredictability. For the decline of the
> great religious monopolies in the West has been accompanied
> by the sporadic deployment of religion for a great variety of
> new purposes. Religion can be combined with virtually any

other set of ideas or values. And the chances that religion will be controversial are increased by the fact that it may be used by people having little or no connection with formal religious organisations. The deregulation of religion is one of the hidden ironies of secularisation. It helps to make religion sociologically problematic in ways which are virtually inconceivable in the terms of the sociological classics.'[32]

This summarises very well a change of perception that is clearly taking place amongst sociologists of religion themselves. It is a change that could with benefit be noted by Christian ethicists, even though they might regard it as a matter of debate whether religion really has changed so radically or whether instead there have always been tensions within religions which the 'founding fathers' in sociology chose to ignore. Be that as it may, it is clear that there is a new voice sounding within the sociology of religion. Neither Durkheim's functionalism nor Wilson's epiphenomenalism prevail. The social significance of religions is taken seriously, but not as some unitary, essentially conservative, force. It is now more widely maintained that religions can induce moral conformity, but they can also provoke moral protest and dissent. They can bind and they can divide. And even in apparently secular worlds religious factors can still be potent. Even dangerous.

[32] ibid., pp. 171–2.

7
Theology and the Nuclear Debate

And the most dangerous area may be this. In recent years the task of doing Christian ethics in secular worlds has been particularly influential in the debate about nuclear issues. Manifestly the nuclear industry raises ethical issues. If once it might have been thought right for scientists to be 'pure scientists', pursuing empirical research wherever it might lead and ignoring the uses that might be made of the products of their research, today in a nuclear age such stances have become distinctly less morally credible. There seems a growing acceptance that scientists ought not to remain 'morally neutral'. It is not thought sufficient for them to work disinterestedly on weapons of mass destruction or to ignore the consequences to the environment of nuclear energy. If their work is to retain public credibility, they are increasingly expected to defend the social consequences of their research as well as the research itself. And, in the process, they become involved in ethics.

For the last decade Churches and theologians have been particularly active in this debate. A whole series of reports and individual contributions have sought to understand the empirical complexities of nuclear weapon systems, nuclear strategies and nuclear industries, and then to relate them to Christian ethics. Few other secular worlds have received such sustained attention by Christian ethicists and few other debates in Christian ethics have proved so socially significant. In Britain *The Church and the Bomb*,[1] produced by a working party of the Church of England in 1982, was widely discussed within the Churches,

[1] Hodder and Stoughton 1982.

within Parliament and amongst theologians. In the United States the National Conference of Catholic Bishops' *The Challenge of Peace: God's Promise and Our Response*,[2] which first appeared in the following year, also received widespread attention.

However, the debate engendered by these two influential documents soon showed that there were deep divisions between Christians on most of the ethical issues involved. If they had hoped for unanimity, it has proved elusive. In this chapter I will try to show that there are good theological reasons for this. Built into the New Testament, and acting as independent variables surfacing when least expected within Christian ethics, are theological barbs which make for an uncomfortable ride in this particular secular world.

I

Peacemaking in a Nuclear Age[3] provides an instructive example. It was published in July 1988 by a working party of the Board for Social Responsibility of the General Synod of the Church of England, bringing together theologians and military experts who notoriously disagree on the propriety of possessing, let alone using, nuclear weapons. Chaired by Richard Harries, the Bishop of Oxford, the balance of the working party was clearly in favour of defenders of nuclear deterrence. Nonetheless it did also include critics such as Rowan Williams.

It was a deliberate attempt, in the wake of the controversy[4] following *The Church and the Bomb*, to reflect and then resolve differences on these crucial issues. In his introduction, Harries described the method adopted as follows:

> 'The Working Party reflects diverse views on the issues and this has been valuable. One of our members is not a Christian but has been happy to share in this task because of the seriousness and importance of its subject-matter. No less important has been the variety of expertise that has been brought to the task, historical, diplomatic, strategic, military,

[2] SPCK 1983.
[3] Church House Publishing 1988.
[4] See Francis Bridger (ed.) *The Cross and the Bomb*, Mowbrays 1983; my *The Cross Against the Bomb*, Epworth 1984; and John Gladwin (ed.), *Dropping the Bomb: The Church and the Bomb Debate*, Hodder and Stoughton 1985.

economic, theological and ethical. The process of working has been as important to us as the result, and offers, we believe, *a model for the Church as a whole and for a broader process of dialogue*. Each draft has been successively modified by the comments of members of the group so that, *despite our different starting points, a real degree of unity has been achieved*.'[5] (my italics)

There is indeed a serious level of realism and sophistication within the report. Its contributors were amongst the most distinguished in this area. Further, it concluded with a convincing series of points on which there appeared to be a growing convergence on nuclear issues within Churches. It concluded: that Christians have a real contribution to make to the process of peacemaking; that nuclear deterrence is not a long-term prescription for stability and peace; that the arms race and new weapon systems carry real dangers for the world; and that comprehensive disarmament must be pursued more vigorously by both East and West.

Nevertheless, before the end of the year a rather different book, *Theology Against the Nuclear Horizon*[6] edited by Alan Race, was published. This book had a quite different group of distinguished theological contributors. They were united instead by the belief that the current nuclear situation is both exceedingly dangerous and fragile and needs to be radically challenged. And they were all concerned to write theology that takes this situation fully into account. As a result it was a considerably more partisan book than the first – but perhaps for this reason distinctly more coherent and challenging.

Amongst the contributors of this second book, Peter Selby, Christopher Rowland and Mark Corner offered theological accounts of a nuclear world in the light of the disturbing notions of Christian apocalyptic. And Alan Race contributed a pointed critique of *Peacemaking in a Nuclear Age*. If the authors of the latter had imagined that the time had arrived when a consensus might be reached amongst Christians on nuclear issues, *Theology Against the Nuclear Horizon* soon demonstrated that they were wrong.

[5] *Peacemaking in a Nuclear Age*, pp. vi–vii.
[6] SCM Press 1988.

This is not the place here to review all of the ethical issues which divide the two books. The arguments, although important, have been rehearsed so often elsewhere,[7] and would in any case soon occupy the rest of my book. Rather it is the theological differences between them which will be noted here. Theology is in the very title of the book edited by Alan Race and in the subtitle of *Peacemaking in a Nuclear Age: A Theological Essay on Deterrence*. For both books, then, theology is crucial to the debate. Yet theology also quite clearly divides them.

Fundamental to the argument of the authors of *Peacemaking in a Nuclear Age* is that 'pax' (defined as 'when war is absent but coercion may be implicit or latent') is as specifically a Christian resource as both 'shalom' and 'inner peace'. Pax even receives the most space in the Report. The authors argued that 'some of the acrimony in the debate about peace in recent years has been due to the simple (or wilful) confusion of different kinds of peace . . . Three main types of peace need to be distinguished and related to one another'.[8] The first of these is the Jewish notion of 'shalom': this 'is not just the peace of solitary individuals but the peace of the whole community . . . It embraces life in its totality, inward and outward, personal, social, political, economic and environmental . . . where there is Shalom, all that is indicated by true justice is present'.[9]

The third type of peace is 'inner peace', which 'is, in essence, a fruit of the union of the human will with the divine will'. Thus, 'the Christian faith offers an inner peace which is not be accounted for wholly in sociological or psychological terms. It offers an inner peace that is a personal participation in Shalom; a fragmentary anticipation, by a particular individual, of that

---

[7] See Roger Ruston, *Nuclear Deterrence – Right or Wrong?*, Catholic Information Service 1981; Francis Bridger (ed.) *The Cross and the Bomb* and my *The Cross Against the Bomb*, op. cit.; Anthony Kenny, *The Logic of Deterrence*, Firethorn 1985; Howard Davis (ed.), *Ethics and Defence: Power and Responsibility in a Nuclear Age*, Blackwells 1986, Richard Harries, *Christianity and War in a Nuclear Age*, Mowbrays 1986; Myron S. Augsburger and Dean C. Curry, *Nuclear Arms: Two Views of World Peace*, World Books, Waco 1987; John Finnis, Joseph M. Boyle and Germain Grisez, *Nuclear Deterrence, Morality and Realism*, Clarendon 1987; Oliver O'Donovan, *Peace and Certainty: A Theological Essay on Deterrence*, Clarendon 1989.

[8] op. cit., p. 1.

[9] ibid., pp. 1–2.

Divine peace which one day will embrace the whole of existence'.[10]

But it is the second type of peace which is described at greatest length and which is most used in the report that follows. In summary form, the authors argued as follows:

> 'Shalom is such a heady notion it is easy for theologians to overlook the vital need for Pax. Any country that has known war on its own soil, or which has been beset by civil strife, knows the great blessing of a simple cessation of hostilities. There is . . . a bedrock meaning of peace, the simple absence of war . . .'

> 'It is difficult to find a definition of Pax which does not assume either that all Pax is coercive or that no coercion is present. The definition chosen here *Pax: when war is absent* but *coercion may be implicit or latent* does not seek to prejudice any issue, simply to reflect the fact that a state of "absence of war" may be one in which goodwill and economic co-operation are basic to the relationship and coercion is minimal or one in which war is kept at bay only by the mutual fear of the consequences of going to war. Societies are held together by a mixture of coercion and consent.'[11]

The authors admitted frankly that this concept of pax assumes that 'coercion, overt or implicit, is a permanent feature of sinful human existence. Individuals, groups and nations have an ineluctable tendency to pursue their own interests without taking the interests of others into account'.[12] Hence the need for nuclear deterrence in a sinful world: coercion is built into the concept of pax.

Once this notion of pax was accepted as a (perhaps *the*) primary Christian resource, the rest of the report followed quite logically. But suppose, instead, that pax is regarded as essentially a sub-Christian notion. Clearly it owes more to the Roman world, appearing almost indistinguishable from the notion of *pax romana*, than it does to the New Testament. Even those Christian ethicists who have argued that a notion of *pax romana* is implicit in the New Testament, have typically done so on the

[10] ibid., p. 8.
[11] ibid., pp. 3 and 5.
[12] ibid., p. 6.

basis of arguments from silence[13] (e.g. Jesus did not actually condemn soldiers), not from any explicit evidence. Viewed in this context pax might be regarded, like abortion, as ubiquitous in a secular society but not as on that account a Christian notion. It would indeed be very difficult to make sense of liturgical uses of pax in terms of the definition of the report. *Pax vobiscum* surely has little to do with the absence of war based upon potential coercion. But having adopted such a sub-Christian notion of pax, it is perhaps not surprising that the authors seldom emphasised the extreme danger and fragility of the present nuclear situation. And the report contained only seven-and-a-half ambivalent pages on the morality of nuclear deterrence. And, most surprisingly of all, it even offered theological support for a first use nuclear policy.

All of this is in stark contrast to the theological positions underlying *Theology Against the Nuclear Horizon*. In his analysis of *peacemaking in a Nuclear Age*, Alan Race argued that 'we must not forget the critique which *shalom* offers to *pax*, especially when Christians and theologians are drawn into the spell of international politics. In the report, the balance between compromise and critique, tips firmly in the former's favour'.[14] And herein lies the problem. Theology no longer seriously challenges the nuclear status quo:

> 'In the context of the processes of seeking arms control, human rights, and detente – highly laudable aims in themselves – pursuing peace is dependent on some sense of durability in our world, some sense of underlying continuity under the umbrella of nuclear "defence". Yet it is precisely this sense of durability which is under threat, and which requires us to rethink the meaning of defence and any theology which may be related to it. Under such circumstances theology ought to place before us the real choice: either acquiescent and *pax*-minded co-operation with the philosophy of nuclear "defence" and arms control, or Christian and *shalom*-minded resistance as a form of radical response to the changed conditions in a nuclear world.'[15]

[13] See further my *A Textbook of Christian Ethics*, T&T Clark 1985.
[14] op. cit., p. 172.
[15] op. cit., p. 173.

Admittedly writing in 1988 not in 1991, Race concluded that 'behind the odd breakthrough in East–West relations nothing much fundamentally has changed . . . the nuclear arms race has achieved a life of its own, and . . . theology deserves a better visionary profile that what has been offered here'.[16] Although in the 1990s there has been a far more dramatic breakthrough in East–West relations, the nuclear arms race still continues apace. Both vertical and horizontal nuclear proliferations persist. That is to say, nuclear weapons continuously become more sophisticated and dangerous, permeate more and more levels of strategic command, and are possessed by an ever-growing group of nations. East–West relations, as the Gulf War has clearly shown, are now just one level of the nuclear issue. In this broader context, Race's point about theological critique is still relevant.

A very similar point has been made recently by Oliver O'Donovan in his *Peace and Certainty: A Theological Essay on Deterrence*.[17] He is suspicious of the Niebuhrian 'realism' that underlies so many of Harries' own arguments[18] on nuclear defence and which clearly shaped *Peacemaking in a Nuclear Age*. O'Donovan argues instead for a concept of peace which is first and foremost christological and eschatological:

'Christian striving for peace arises within this eschatological horizon, on the basis of God's gift once given, in the hope of a promise that is not vague but precisely determined. The presence of Jesus as Lord is the reality which we know and the shape of the future for which we hope. The point at issue between political "idealism" and political "realism" is not, as was influentially claimed by Reinhold Niebuhr half a century ago, the doctrine of original sin. It is simply Jesus as Lord. The point at issue is Christological: whether it is the peace *which God has given* that determines the peace which we seek, and which therefore forbids us to fashion for ourselves an unreal goal of ultimate peace which is no more than the projection of unsatisfied human longings.'[19]

[16] op. cit., p. 174.
[17] Clarendon 1989.
[18] See Harries' essay in Bridger, op. cit., and Richard Harries (ed.), *Reinhold Niebuhr and the Issues of Our Time*, Mowbrays 1986.
[19] op. cit., pp. 114–15.

It is precisely at this point that theology can be seen to be an uncomfortable barb in the nuclear debate. If Christians are sometimes tempted to believe that the social function of religion is simply to bind society together, along the lines already criticised, O'Donovan and the contributors to *Theology Against the Nuclear Horizon* act as stark reminders that this is not necessarily so. Theology can also challenge and disrupt the *status quo*. Or, to express this more sociologically, theology can at times act as an independent social variable. Furthermore, within the context of the nuclear debate, it is the eschatological and indeed apocalyptic features of the New Testament that have recently played such a major role in this disruption.

2

Ironically it is passages such as Mark 13 that have shaped these theological arguments. Within critical theology a generation ago it was widely assumed that the apocalyptic features of the New Testament required explanation rather than sympathetic reading. Even the otherwise theologically conservative scholar G. R. Beasley-Murray[20] concluded that parts of Mark 13 belonged to the mistaken assumptions about the end of the world of early Christians, and possibly of Jesus himself. Of course, other conservative theologians never concurred with this judgement. Adventist sectarians, and now parts of the new religious right, continued to believe in an imminent earthly parousia, albeit still arguing about the specific timing of this parousia.[21]

However, under the threat of nuclear extinction, critical theologians began to look at New Testament apocalypticism in a far more positive manner. There were the strange and disturbing chapters in Jim Garrison's *The Darkness of God*[22] which attempted to produce a synthesis of Hiroshima and apocalyptic. There have been the hints offered by the Christian ethicist and radical pacifist, Stanley Hauerwas. And Moltmann has sometimes made a specific, and by no means entirely negative,

[20] G. R. Beasley Murray, *Jesus and the Future*, London 1954, and *A Commentary on Mark Thirteen*, London 1957.

[21] See further Roger Ruston, 'Apocalyptic and the Peace Movement', *New Blackfriars* 67, 791, May 1986.

[22] SCM Press 1982.

connection between Christian apocalyptic and nuclear/ environmental disaster. Although all avoided the crude assimilations of futurology and apocalypticism of some sectarians, and indeed have a profound distaste for the writings of the new religious right, they no longer dismissed apocalypticism as simply anachronistic.

The dangers here are obvious and few depict them better than Moltmann. In *The Crucified God*[23] he was deeply critical of sectarian apocalyptic and saw it as an obvious temptation for the present-day churches:

> 'Christians, churches and theologians who passionately defend true belief, pure doctrine and distinctive Christian morality are at the present day in danger of lapsing into this pusillanimous faith. Then they build a defensive wall round their own little group, and in apocalyptic terms call themselves the "little flock" or the "faithful remnant", and abandon the world outside to the godlessness and immorality which they themselves lament. They lament the assimilation of Christianity to the secularised society which has declined since the "good old days", and bewail the loss of identity of those who in theology and in practice involve themselves in the conflicts of this society and work with others to resolve them. But by this reaction, they themselves are running the risk of a loss of identity by passive assimilation. They accept the increasing isolation of the church as an insignificant sect on the margin of society, and encourage it by their sectarian withdrawal. The symptoms of the increase of this kind of sectarian mentality at the present day include the preservation of tradition without the attempt to found new tradition; biblicism without liberating preaching; increasing unwillingness to undergo new experience with the gospel and faith, and the language of zealotry and militant behaviour in disputes within the church.'[24]

This general form of sectarianism can be found in a very specific form amongst those Christian groups who see apocalypticism and disasters as part of some discernible divine plan. Moltmann argued forcefully that this is a misunderstanding of Christian apocalyptic:

[23] SCM Press 1974.
[24] ibid., p. 20.

'In this post-Christian, legalistic apocalyptic, the present time becomes the moment of the great decision: the world is lapsing into the spiritual death of atheism, atomic catastrophe, the death of the young from drugs or ecological self-destruction. At the same time, it is the hour in which the true church has to rise up as the visible place of refuge in the disaster: "Rise up for the final struggle." It cannot be denied that such visions of the future exist in the New Testament, and that the crises of history may come to such a critical end. But nowhere in the New Testament does the "end of the world" bring about the second coming of Christ. The New Testament looks forward to the very reverse, that the second coming of Christ will bring the end of destruction and persecution in the world. Anyone who reads the "signs of the time" with the eyes of his own existential anxiety reads them falsely. If they can be read at all, they can be read by Christians only with the eyes of hope in the future of Christ. Otherwise the apocalyptic interpretations of the age will be like the nihilistic attempt of the "devils" of Dostoevsky, who want to destroy the world in order to force God to intervene, and who for romantic reasons regard chaos itself as creative. But this no longer has anything to do with the cross as the horizon of the world, for this cross is the sign of the unity of love for God and the love with which, according to the Gospel of John (3:16), God "so loved the world, that he gave his only Son".'[25]

It is clear from this that Moltmann himself is firmly in what Roger Ruston[26] has termed the 'optimistic' group of apocalypticists. It also becomes clear that he (like Christopher Rowland)[27] does not treat apocalyptic as a phenomenon which is *sui generis* or even a single phenomenon: 'Apocalyptic is a syncretistic formation with more than one idea. But at its centre we do not find anthropology or universal history, but the expectation of the future victory of the righteousness of God over dead and living. The "resurrection of the dead" has no significance of its own, but is thought of as a *conditio sine qua non* for the universal achievement of righteousness in the judgement upon righteous and unrighteous.'[28]

[25] ibid., p. 21.
[26] See n. 21.
[27] See Christopher Rowland, *The Open Heaven: A Study of Apocalyptic in Judaism and Early Christianity*, SPCK 1982.
[28] Moltmann, op. cit., p. 177.

In general terms this seems to correspond with Rowland's claim that apocalyptic involves a radical stress on the 'vertical'. In terms of Jesus' own proclamation, Moltmann insisted that it was 'apocalyptic in form, as far as, like John the Baptist, he proclaimed the imminence of the distant kingdom ... The scandal was not the message that one man had been raised before all others in the final judgement and the kingdom of God, but the certainty that this one man was the crucified Jesus'.[29]

To these two concepts of the 'vertical' and 'imminence' Moltmann added a third, concerned with 'triumph': 'The message of the new righteousness which eschatological faith brings into the world says that in fact the executioners will not finally triumph over their victims. It also says that in the end their victims will not triumph over their executioners. The one will triumph who first died for the victims and then also for the executioners, and in so doing revealed a new righteousness which breaks through the vicious circles of hate and vengeance and which for the lost victims and executioners creates a new mankind with a new humanity.'[30]

These three concepts – the 'vertical', 'imminence', and final 'triumph' – are all clearly present in Mark 13 (although not in the Pauline terms in which Moltmann presented them). Together with two other concepts present in Mark 13 – 'fragility' and 'unknownness' – they have struck chords in a number of theologians involved in the peace/environmental movement. The 'fragility' is evident at the beginning of the chapter, in that the whole proclamation is set in the context of a political/social order which is seen as essentially fragile. The 'unknownness' occurs at the end (vs 32).

All of these elements are evident at various points in the writings and lectures of Charles Elliott. After all his very considerable work in development economics and his attempt to direct Christian Aid it would be difficult to put him in anything but the Ruston 'optimistic' group. And this despite his present bleakness. *Praying the Kingdom*[31] is, in part, a bleak and discouraging book, but it concluded with an emphasis upon the

[29] ibid.
[30] ibid., p. 178.
[31] DLT 1985.

effectiveness of prayer and a Franciscan style of spirituality. Indeed, he accused theological liberals of having lost confidence in the effectiveness of prayer and of believing that 'just' praying is 'doing' nothing.

Praying the Kingdom contains most of the five features of apocalyptic just noted. The imminence of catastrophe (both nuclear and environmental) dominates the early chapters, as does the fragility of the individual caught up in the dual situation of guilt and powerlessness. And elsewhere he has identified the institutions of political/social oppression responsible for creating the powerlessness, referred to earlier in Chapter 3, as the Beast of Revelation.[32] It is clear from this and from the stress upon prayer for the Kingdom as the only solution offered in the book, that the 'vertical' and 'triumph' features are also important for Elliott. *Praying the Kingdom* might even appear to some as excessively pietistic and utopian (albeit other-worldly utopianism). Were it not for Elliott's utter seriousness, almost desperation as one who has tried and failed to change world poverty (itself inextricably bound up with world armaments), it would be easy to dismiss his use of apocalyptic language as 'poetic' language. Were it not for his obvious left-wing stance and his critical/analytical powers, it would be easy to identify him with more conservative and fundamentalist understandings of apocalyptic. But both of these interpretations would be profoundly wrong. He is serious: he is critical: he is 'unknowing': but he has also been deeply influenced by New Testament apocalyptic.

Jim Garrison offers a more difficult example. There can be no doubt that he belongs to the Peace Movement (more fully than most) or that he intends to write on apocalyptic from the perspective of critical theology. He offered an earlier and more sustained analysis of the connection than any theologian I know. But at the same time his syntheses is more idiosyncratic than most, as the very title, *The Darkness of God: Theology after Hiroshima*, indicates. He combined his analysis with long sections on Jung and linked the wrath of God to the specific development of nuclear weapons. Finally he looked for new fusions between the human and the divine:

[32] In a lecture given at New College, Edinburgh, in 1985.

'Therefore the synthesis between Hiroshima and apocalyptic challenges us to explore the coming together of humanity and God in our new found powers of global destruction. It is important to stress the co-operative character of the apocalyptic possibilities in our day. Hiroshima humanising the apocalypse means that if the wrath of God must come it is human hands which will push the button; and if the righteousness of God will replace the old order with a new age it is human work which will create it. In history, God never works alone, but always in conjunction with human beings. Therefore, it is imperative to find the locus of the Divine/ human interface within the human realm.'

'Because Hiroshima has humanised the eschaton and for the first time placed the capability to destroy the world in human hands, it is important to discern that locus in which three things occur: first, in which the human realities of darkness and light are felt most strongly; second, in which these human feelings and drives engage with, and are affected by, God; and third, in which some type of synthesis can occur not only between the forces peculiarly human but also between the human and the Divine.'[33]

Critical theologians have often been puzzled by the status of some of Garrison's claims. His writings can be puzzling and disturbing, but they are not simplistic. Apocalypticism is treated seriously, but not uncritically. Like a number of other theologians, the fragile and potentially devastating context of a nuclear age has prompted him to respond to some of the resonances of New Testament apocalypticism. Theological disdain has been replaced by fresh readings of old and disturbing biblical passages.

Implicit within several of these examples of recent use of Christian apocalyptic is a sixth feature, which is certainly present in Mark 13 and much apocalyptic, namely 'judgement'. It is a feature more typical perhaps of some forms of sectarianism and the new religious right, and more troublesome to those in a tradition of critical theology. The difficulty is pin-pointed by the last of my examples, Stanley Hauerwas. Like Moltmann he is first and foremost a theologian and like Elliott his writings are characterised by a strong 'vertical' stress. His writings in

[33] op. cit., p. 119.

Christian ethics, as mentioned in Chapter 1, have proved to be amongst the most important of those seeking to return to a more strictly theological understanding of the discipline. He is always at his most caustic when he is depicting Christian ethicists whose 'Christian' bases are too hidden – for example, in what he has teasingly depicted as 'The Rise (and fall) of Medical Ethics'.[34] In characteristic style he quoted, with obvious approval, A. E. Harvey to the effect that a conviction that an impending catastrophe which can only be averted through a change of heart describes both our current nuclear situation and the situation depicted by early Christian apocalyptic. But then he added to taunt those he depicts as 'liberals':

> 'But some of you may by now have begun to lose patience with all this talk of eschatology and in particular with these last apocalyptic notes. Christian biblical scholars and theologians have spent the last century trying to explain Jesus' and/or the early church's apocalyptic pronouncements in a manner such that we do not have to take them seriously. It seems particularly inopportune to raise them in relation to the issue of nuclear disarmament since they can only further complicate this already complex issue. After all, the world did not come to an end during the generation of the people who knew Jesus, and Christians, like other folk, have had to try ever since to live in a world which seems to go on indefinitely.'[35]

At first glance this might appear to be a plea to return to a non-critical understanding of apocalyptic. But, in fact, Hauerwas has already disallowed this when describing 'those Christians who cannot resist speculating about the imminent end of the world and, perhaps, even co-operating to bring it about'.[36] The paragraph following the one just quoted shows his particular use of apocalyptic in the nuclear context:

> 'But quite to the contrary, Christians are a people who believe that we have, in fact, seen the end; that the world has for all time experienced its decisive crisis in the life and death of Jesus

[34] Stanley Hauerwas, *Suffering Presence*, University of Notre Dame Press 1986, and T&T Clark 1988, p. 1.
[35] Stanley Hauerwas, *Against the Nations: War and Survival in a Liberal Society*, Winston Press 1985, p. 165.
[36] ibid., p. 161.

of Nazareth. For in his death we believe that the history of the universe reached its turning point. At that moment in history, when the decisive conflict between God and the powers took place, our end was resolved in favour of God's lordship over this existence. Through Jesus' cross and resurrection the end has come; the kingdom has been established. Indeed it had to come in such a fashion for it is a kingdom that only God could bring about.'[37]

From these various examples I believe that a picture begins to form. It is clear that a critical use of apocalyptic in the nuclear context is beginning to emerge. The area is fraught with traps and difficulties. Further it is not difficult for a sociologist to suggest why nuclear anxiety tends to breed a renewed interest in apocalyptic. However, I also believe that these examples indicate that some of the strongest features of apocalyptic can be used suggestively within a critical tradition of theology. The very differences within the biblical apocalyptic genre itself mean that the critical theologian inevitably has to be selective. Yet the observation that this genre has contacts and affinities with other genres may render it somewhat more accessible than once appeared.

I have singled out six features which seem to emerge from a passage like Mark 13 and which seem particularly apposite to a nuclear age. 'Imminence' and 'fragility' are both given a fresh twist by an awareness of the increasing proliferation and instability of nuclear armaments. Fundamentalists doubtless tend to see this proliferation and instability as a part of some divine plan made known through apocalyptic revelation. For the critical theologian this is a clear contradiction of the feature of 'unknownness'. It is seen not as a part of a plan but more simply as a part of human beings' present social context which gives an added spur to focus thought on the 'vertical' feature of apocalyptic. In such a dangerous situation people may have an incentive to focus on the 'vertical' and through this on the 'eschaton' or final 'triumph'. Again, the final 'triumph' and the 'judgement' that precedes it are pictured by fundamentalists typically in terms that appear grossly speculative, and perhaps morally repulsive, to the critical apocalypticist. But that the

[37] ibid.

present situation of nuclear proliferation and instability is a judgement upon humans and an affront to the Creator seems only too obvious.

Finally what distinguishes the Christian in the nuclear context is that he or she believes that the world is indeed God-given. A proper response to a gift is not a preparedness to let it be destroyed, let alone to destroy it oneself. Rather the response should be gratitude, responsibility and hope: gratitude because it is not earned or merited; responsibility because it is a gift of love; and hope because the Giver continues a giving relationship in the body of Christ. The hope of final 'triumph' is a theological extrapolation from this gift relationship.

Hauerwas believes that it is this hope which distinguishes an adequate theological approach to apocalyptic either from the secular desire for survival, examined in Chapter 4, or from fundamentalist speculations about the future. Both, 'fail to understand that the Christian expectation of the end can be hopeful only because we know that it is God's future and his decision that will bring it about. If all that stands between us and despair is the prospect of the indefinite continuation of the human species, we indeed live in a hopeless world'.[38]

3

Little of this conforms to the theological vision predominant in *Peacemaking in a Nuclear Age*. Apocalypticism, even in the forms of critical hermeneutics, tends to be barbed and uncomfortable. It is likely to disturb balances of terror carefully constructed in the interests of nuclear deterrence. In the preface to *Peace and Certainty* Oliver O'Donovan records that he made a visit to NATO and thanks NATO staff for their 'frankness and geniality', but then adds at once: 'Needless to say, my views are my own.'[39] The chapters that follow offer little comfort for those upholding the nuclear *status quo* in NATO. The prefaces to Stanley Hauerwas' *The Peaceable Kingdom*[40] and *Against the Nations* mention only academic and ecclesiastical contexts.

[38] ibid., p. 162.
[39] op. cit., p. vii.
[40] University of Notre Dame Press 1983 and SCM Press 1984.

Neither theologian would have been able to contribute much to the 'theological consensus' sought by *Peacemaking in a Nuclear Age* and offered as a 'model' for others in the Churches working in this vexed area.

But perhaps it is a flawed model. Perhaps it attempts to tame and constrain theology in a way that both is unlikely to succeed and misunderstands the nature of the theological task. Christopher Rowland's *Radical Christianity*[41] presents a sharply different model. For Rowland, Christian scriptures, despite differing diachronic and synchronic receptions and interpretations, carry within themselves radical ideas which tend to resurface in unexpected places and at unexpected times. Potent symbols of change are carried often unwittingly by Christian communities. They are, to use my earlier phrase, harbingers of values which they may neither always exemplify nor even wholly understand themselves. Yet they persist. And throughout Christian history, radical forms of Christianity have been shaped by them.

Critics of Rowland have disputed some of his examples of radical Christianity and/or claimed that his selection is too idiosyncratic. However, neither of these criticisms affects his basic thesis. The New Testament manifestly does contain within it radical theological tensions – especially in the area of apocalypticism – and various theologians in the present as well as in the past have responded positively to these tensions. And in such a situation, any abiding theological consensus which seeks to give broad support to international nuclear strategy would seem unlikely. On the contrary, as the world becomes increasingly anxious about ecological and nuclear fragility, so any consensus is more likely to be challenged by radical theological stances.

So Rowland argues:

'The story of Christianity in this and every age is in part a story of the ways in which its symbols have been used by different groups and classes but partly also the extraordinary ambivalence of its scriptures with regard to change in society. In the very process of taming its radical symbols by their incorpora-

[41] Polity Press 1988.

tion into a collection which also included injunctions to political quietism and social conservatism, these potent symbols of change were preserved to be used by those who saw the Beast at large in their own day and needed the encouragement of the foundation documents of the faith to continue the struggle even if it did mean that they would have to follow their own Way of the Cross like the Messiah.'[42]

From a sociological perspective, it may not be too difficult to understand some of the stances adopted within the Churches on nuclear issues over the last decade. Given the established position of the Church of England, it was perhaps entirely predictable that its General Synod would not endorse the radical report *The Church and the Bomb* in February 1983.[43] Frequently cited as an 'excellent debate' (almost as if this in itself were a Christian virtue), its outcome never was seriously in doubt. In contrast, the General Assembly Church of Scotland, with its relative independence from the State, could endorse a unilateralist nuclear position – but even then just briefly. Likewise, viewed sociologically, the emergence of radical apocalypticism amongst a number of recent theologians may be seen as a mark of wider social fragility and ferment.

Obviously neither of these sociological observations invalidates these theological stances. Only those confusing social origins with validity (the genetic fallacy) would imagine otherwise. Instead, together they point to the diverse social roles of Christianity and may act as a warning against simplistic calls for theological unanimity on contentious moral issues.

From a theological perspective, the recent literature that I have surveyed in this chapter strongly suggests that theology, however varied, does affect moral stances. The nuclear debate, like the broader ecological debate, raises crucial issues about the nature of creation and redemption, about the role of human sin, and about eschatological possibilities. Christian ethics in this particular secular world offers disturbing, and perhaps even socially disruptive, visions – visions beyond bare survival and the mere absence of war.

[42] ibid., p. 156.
[43] See further my *Beyond Decline*, SCM Press 1988.

8

Aids and Social Policy

In the previous chapter I examined an issue in which Christian ethicists seem to be increasingly in sharp conflict with secular assumptions. Christian ethics in this particular secular world seems at present to be predominantly drawn to the Hauerwas approach. Apocalyptic symbols have resurfaced challenging secular assumptions about forms of 'peace' which are dependent upon nuclear deterrence. At the most Christian ethicists tend to justify such 'peace' as the lesser of two evils or as a sad but necessary compromise in a fallen world. More frequently they regard with apocalyptic horror world-wide signs of horizontal and vertical nuclear escalation protected by theories of deterrence.

In this chapter, in contrast, I will turn to medical ethics. In this secular world Christian ethics over the last two decades has been remarkably successful. Much of the medical world has responded enthusiastically to ethical categories, even to those deriving from Christian theologians. Theologians such as Alastair Campbell and Jack Mahoney in Britain have made substantial and highly influential contributions to medical ethics. Further, it is now quite normal for medical students and nurses in training to have some formal teaching in ethics. Ethical monitoring committees have become a standard procedure and there are in Britain and the States well established and respected journals of medical ethics. And increasingly medical ethics itself contributes distinctions and concepts to the wider body of professional ethical discussion. Few other professions or secular worlds have taken ethics so seriously.

As a result Christian ethics in this secular world has unusually rich opportunities for dialogue. However, for those who wish to take part in this dialogue it has usually become a prerequisite that faith commitments, whilst not irrelevant, should not be used to exclude those with differing faith commitments. Christian ethicists are still welcome within many medical ethics circles, but are encouraged to tread carefully.

By now it will be clear that I do believe that this is often (but not always) a legitimate role for Christian ethics. Christian ethicists in secular worlds do not always have to challenge stridently and to denounce. In medical ethics it is usually more appropriate that we should listen, explore and prompt. This, I believe, is especially important in the vexed moral area to be considered in this chapter. There have been a few egregious examples of Christian 'challenges' to AIDS sufferers. Fortunately they have usually been outweighed by those more inspired by Christian care and compassion.

As mentioned earlier, this chapter is different in style from the other chapters since it is written in the form of a report. However its intentions are similar. Whatever the empirical and social problems involved in looking at AIDS and social policy, those of us responsible for the report (for details see the Preface and Introduction) are all convinced that ethical reflection here is vital. And the others in the group have been remarkably tolerant of the fact that it has always been a theologian who chairs it.

THE REPORT

(1) As a working party we have frequently noted that ethical discussions of AIDS policies have tended to focus upon the rights of individuals and less upon the well-being, or common good, of society at large. So there has been considerable discussion of the issues of confidentiality, non-discrimination against individuals who are HIV positive, the legal and financial rights of those in this group, and the need to educate through persuasion of individuals rather than through social coercion. A select bibliography is attached to the end of this report. Furthermore, individual AIDS sufferers have been the recipients of preferential medical services in Britain which are largely confidential, in the North East at least, even from most GPs.

(2) We do not wish to detract from this ethical emphasis. On the

contrary, we are impressed with the way those from the health service working with AIDS sufferers, voluntary caring agencies, self-help groups of AIDS sufferers, church groups, and many others have shown real care and moral sensitivity in this vexed area. Sometimes they have acted in this way despite considerable prejudice and fear in the public at large.

(3) Nevertheless, we are convinced that a wider moral perspective is also necessary. AIDS concerns society as a whole and raises crucial issues concerned with the common good. A notion of the 'common good' is not simply concerned with the will of the majority (as in forms of utilitarianism). It is also concerned with caring for disadvantaged minorities. In this sense it is an altruistic concept treating people less as isolated individuals than as persons-in-community – persons, that is, with what have been aptly termed 'complementary interests'. Common good is 'common' precisely because it embraces both the good of individuals and the good of different groups, as they contribute to each other and to the well-being of society as a whole.

(4) We have deliberately focused upon the ethics of social policies related to AIDS for several reasons:

(i) In the expectation that AIDS will become considerably more widespread in society over the next few decades.

(ii) that prostitution, drug abuse and especially prisons (all areas already involving social policy) may well be the primary agencies through which AIDS spreads into the heterosexual population.

(iii) that, as this happens, so there may be increasing pressure from the general public to enforce more drastic social policies.

(iv) In the belief that the ethical consequences of these policies should be thought out clearly in advance of these pressures.

(5) It should be possible to list policy options according to their degree of ethical difficulty and/or complexity. Most of these policy options involve some degree of preferential resource allocation – itself having ethical implications – so these are treated first. Three broad areas of policy option can be distinguished:

- the first of these concerns health education and health promotion.
- the second involves information gathering: as AIDS becomes more widespread so increasingly intrusive methods of information gathering may be called for by the public at large.
- the third area of policy option involves preventive action with various degrees of social coercion.

(6) It will become apparent that setting out policy options in this way does at times reveal increasing conflicts between what are often perceived as the ethical rights of individuals and the needs of society at large. Any balance between a concern for individual rights and a concern for the well-being of society at large is likely to involve some degree of ethical conflict. However, it should also be stressed that a notion of the 'common good' suggests that so-called 'individual rights' should always be viewed in the larger context of persons-in-community and of complementary interests. The object of listing policy options in this way would be to provide both a means of predicting the sort of options society is increasingly likely to consider as AIDS spreads, and to provide a means for assessing these policy options ethically.

(7) At a sociological level the spread of AIDS may be divided into at least three broad phases. Although in practice they may overlap somewhat (with marked regional variations), they are distinct as broad phases. Each of these depends upon social perception:

- In the *first phase* AIDS is widely seen as a problem involving homosexuals, drug addicts and haemophiliacs. It is not seen by the bulk of the heterosexual population as an issue that directly concerns them or which should seriously modify their own behaviour. Until recently this was probably the social perception of AIDS widely prevalent in Britain.
- In the *second phase* AIDS is more widely perceived to be a problem which does involve heterosexuals. In this phase AIDS might be seen by most heterosexuals as a disease which should marginally alter their own behaviour (e.g. by increasing the use of condoms), but not as a disease which

requires more drastic policy options. There are clear signs
that Britain is now moving into this phase, with the fastest
growing group of recent cases of HIV infection being
amongst heterosexuals.

- In the *third phase* most heterosexuals will know someone
personally who is HIV Positive, or, more significantly, who
has died from AIDS. In addition to widespread adult
infection, in this phase babies will also increasingly be born
with HIV infection. Countries such as Zambia have
probably already reached this phase. However even conservative estimates about the spread of AIDS suggest that by
1993 Britain will be unambiguously in the second phase (and
that parts of Edinburgh may already be in it) and moving
into the third. It is our belief that as this third phase
approaches in Britain, so there will be increasing social
pressure to introduce policy options in the interests of
society at large which conflict with the ethical rights of
individuals and of minorities.

(8) PREFERENTIAL RESOURCE ALLOCATION

Advertising and public information require funding, as indeed do
all of the policy options which follow. Because of the public and
political unease about AIDS it very quickly became established
that there would be a preferential allocation of resources in this
area. Currently AIDS sufferers receive a highly preferential
pattern of medical care and sizeable amounts of health resources
are being spent in an attempt to limit the spread of AIDS. Whilst
few might object to all of this, it is not wholly without ethical
problems. Resource allocation clearly involves priorities, and if
priority is given to one group or one disease or disability then it
may at the same time be denied to others. In the present context
of GPs, health authorities and hospitals becoming more conscious of limited budgets, arguments within and between them
about this preferential resource allocation will we suspect
increase in the near future.

On the other hand, public unease about the threat of AIDS,
even as perceived in *Phase One*, may in itself be considered
sufficient to justify present (and perhaps in *Phase Two* an
increasing) resource allocation in this area. One of the criteria

which determines resource allocation in health services may well be (and perhaps should be) current public perceptions and fears. In *Phase Three* there may be fresh problems. As the infection becomes more widespread, preferential resource allocation may be viewed as an increasing burden upon the health services – especially if treatment remains fairly ineffective.

(9) HEALTH EDUCATION AND PROMOTION

(i) *Education* – the earliest political responses to AIDS in *Phase One* have mostly involved education in the form of advertising and public information. At several points this response has conflicted with the perceived individual rights of some, since advertising has sometimes been thought to be offensive, practices such as anal intercourse have received more public expression than hitherto, and the emphasis has been upon 'safe', or more accurately 'safer' sex (the so-called 'condom culture'), and 'safer' drug taking, and less upon abstinence or corporate responsibility.

There has clearly been an attempt in much of the health education on AIDS to avoid 'moralising', both because it might be ineffective and because there is no single sexual morality which is seen to command the support of society at large. Groups (and even churches) have divided views on sexual morality, so, not surprisingly, health authorities generally resist adopting partisan positions in this area. In addition, those working directly with AIDS sufferers are rightly cautious about alienating their clients on the issue of sexual morality.

Nevertheless, we have persistently noticed an asymmetry in some of the health education literature that has come to our attention. There are few compunctions about 'moralising' about alcohol consumption, eating habits, smoking, solvent abuse, drugs, or even dental care. These forms of 'moralising' persist even when their effectiveness in vulnerable groups is doubted (e.g. on smoking) or when they run counter to popular culture (e.g. on alcohol consumption). Furthermore, to adopt a campaign that promotes condom use is not itself morally neutral: implicit within it may be an acceptance that people cannot, will not, or perhaps should not, drastically change their sexual practices.

There may also be empirical grounds for doubting the wisdom

of this campaign. Firstly, condoms are amongst the least popular forms of contraceptive, and are soon rejected by groups (or resisted by them altogether) when other options are available. Not surprisingly, then, there are now signs that health education in this area is failing to convince even at-risk groups. Secondly, condoms are not wholly reliable either as contraceptives or as protections against the HIV virus. In the context of anal intercourse, some estimates suggest that two-out-of-five conventional condoms burst.

As a policy, health education has been particularly effective amongst haemophiliacs and, initially at least, amongst male homosexuals. But, despite some important evidence about changes of behaviour amongst older prostitutes, it would appear to have been least effective in precisely those groups through which AIDS may spread into the heterosexual population (see 3(ii)), and even relatively ineffective amongst the young and possibly decreasingly effective amongst male homosexuals.

(ii) *Promotion* – some health authorities have combined education with health promotion – e.g. by making condoms and needles more freely available. The general conflict with the individual rights of some, and perhaps the common good, that result from this policy are broadly similar to those involved in education. However a policy of universal supply would involve additional conflicts even at the social level, since prisoners have notably been so far excluded, despite the very real threat that they represent in terms of the spread of AIDS into the heterosexual population.

There is a clear conflict here between a public policy of punishment (which does not encourage sexual or illegal drug-induced gratification) and the health interests of society at large. It may only be in *Phase Three* that a policy of universal supply will be fully implemented, with considerations of the health of society outweighing existing policies of punishment in prisons.

(10) INFORMATION GATHERING

One of the most important sources of information gathering about HIV infection involves surveys attempting to establish its prevalence. Since these may be anonymous or not and patients may or may not be allowed to opt-out, several broad categories may be distinguished. It should be stressed that these are broad categories, since the concepts of anonymity/non-anonymity and opting-out/non-opting-out can be divided into further sub-types.

Thus tests could be effectively anonymous, but still coded in such a way as to make identification of patients possible in the future. Or they could be coded to make them permanently anonymous. And opting-out could take the form either of asking all patients (either on the first occasion or on each occasion) specifically whether or not they wish to opt out. Or it could simply involve, say, posting a notice in a public place to the effect that patients had the right to opt-out. A further distinction must be made depending upon the issue of for whose benefit the information is gathered – the patient's, the doctor's or the general public's.

Three types of screening are currently practised:

(i) *Voluntary Screening*: Under voluntary arrangement individuals are informed that screening will occur, that they are at liberty to refuse, and that they will be informed as to the result. This occurs with blood donors. However, such individuals are unrepresentative of the population as a whole or those at potential risk. Attempts to undertake broader screening in the interests of the general public by this method have been attempted in the USA, but have failed because of the high refusal rate of those at greatest potential risk.

(ii) *Involuntary Screening*: Under involuntary arrangements patients are not specifically informed that they are to be screened for HIV infection, but blood is used for this purpose and patients are told the result. Such involuntary screening may form part of the diagnostic work-up of a patient suffering from symptoms and signs that might be due to HIV infection (e.g. generalised lymphadenopathy and weight loss). Such patients might however be suffering from another, equally fatal, disease (e.g. disseminated malignancy) and exclusion of these causes also forms part of the diagnostic process. HIV testing in this context is no different from any other diagnostic procedure which might yield information of very serious consequences to the patient. It is not part of conventional clinical practice to itemise the possible consequences of each diagnostic test (unless patients specifically ask) since the patient may ultimately be shown to have a benign condition.

Involuntary screening, on an opportunistic basis (e.g. as is now routine for all patients undergoing haemodialysis), whilst important for the patient and doctor, would be unreliable for epidemiological purposes.

However, involuntary screening is not without ethical difficulties. Patients, could of course still have the right to opt-out of this procedure altogether, but surgeons, in turn, would have the right to refuse to operate on such patients. Such tests might involve conflicts over individual rights – since doctors would have to decide whether or not to divulge information to patients should they prove to be HIV positive. If they did not divulge they would clearly be withholding information from the patients, but if they did they would be involving the patients in all of the social and insurance disabilities attached to HIV/AIDS sufferers.

(iii) *Anonymous Unlinked Screening*: In this procedure, the result of a recent change in Government policy, screening is carried out in patients from part of a particular group in whom blood sampling will be undertaken for another purpose. Additional blood is withdrawn and tested anonymously without the patient's knowledge or active consent. Since screening is carried out anonymously, positive results cannot be ascribed to individuals, and hence they cannot be informed of their HIV infection. This approach has scientific validity when carried out in appropriate groups (e.g. all pregnant patients attending a specific maternity unit) and can yield valuable epidemiological information. Such testing is obviously vital for more accurate epidemiological information upon which future policies might be based.

However, this form of screening does seem to conflict with the rights of individuals since the tests are anonymous (albeit allowing individuals to opt out initially on request) and unlinked, so the information from them thus cannot be passed back to those tested. Unlike most other forms of screening it does not, whilst there is no cure for AIDS at present, have as its raison d'etre detection for treatment. It is also possible that an active process of asking patients if they wish to opt out might, if that practice was widely followed, both distort the results (especially if those from a particularly vulnerable group disproportionately opt out) and raise unforeseen fears in some patients. If, in contrast, the policy is not to ask patients whether or not they wish to opt, but simply to post, say, a notice, then other ethical problems arise. For example, it is presumably only the most literate who usually read such notices, so most might remain unaware of their rights in this area. And does such a policy really amount to patient consent?

(iv) *Non-anonymous, non-opt-out Tests*: When *Phase Three* is reached there might be increasing pressure to remove any op-out clauses and unlinking procedures. Tests could be traced back to specific patients, would be routinely carried out on all blood samples, and no one would have the right to opt-out. Such a scenario would involve some of the features of contact tracing and notification, and would involve a considerable diminution of individual rights in order to protect medical and nursing personnel and society at large. However, it is worth remembering that analogous situations have arisen in the past. Measures to arrest the spread of Hepatitis B have involved similar infringements of individual rights, as have measures to control venereal diseases. Indeed, it may be a continuing oddity of present AIDS policy that it places the rights of individuals before public interests, or the common good, in ways not characteristic of other medical attempts to control the spread of serious infections.

(11) PREVENTIVE ACTION

As the threat of HIV infection increases, moving from *Phase Two* to *Phase Three*, so the following attempts at prevention may well be considered:

(i) *Contact Tracing* – in the context of other sexually transmitted diseases, or more accurately diseases which are transmitted mainly through sexual contact, contact tracing is very important. Of course it raises acute problems of confidentiality and it risks alienating sufferers from presenting themselves to doctors. However the needs of both society and individual contacts are usually thought to act as a counterbalance to the rights of individual sufferers.

Contact tracing in the AIDS context raises two additional ethical problems. Firstly, unlike other forms of sexually transmitted disease there is as yet no cure and thus no substantial benefit to those contacted. At best there is only temporary amelioration (although of course this might change in the future). The aims of contact tracing would primarily be concerned with limiting the spread of HIV infection. And secondly, there is, at least currently, such a public stigma attached to AIDS that those contacted might feel themselves to be more disadvantaged than they would have been had they not been contacted. On the other hand, some of those contacted might as a result feel the need drastically to change their sexual behaviour.

(ii) *Notification* – there may be increasing pressure to make HIV infection a notifiable disease. Clearly this would raise serious ethical problems for patients. The issues of anonymity and confidentiality would again be raised. Statutory notification required of doctors would also seek to place the needs of society as a whole over the rights of the individual patient. In addition, such notification raises the question 'For what purpose is this information required?' If it is required for epidemiological reasons alone, then some of the tests already examined might raise fewer ethical problems. It could also be argued that compulsory notification is unnecessarily coercive and that voluntary notification should be given longer to work. Yet, there is at present a tension, even within official positions, between a belief that a voluntary system works better in Britain than in most other countries, and knowledge from local reviews that nevertheless not even all AIDS cases are in fact reported to the Communicable Disease Surveillance Centre.

(iii) *Penal Policy* – apart from the supply of condoms and needles to prisoners there may be increasing pressure, especially in *Phase Three*, for a radical change of penal policy. Overcrowding in prisons makes anal intercourse and needle sharing almost impossible to control. The threat of the spread of HIV infection might encourage a radical change of penal policy: building more adequate prisons, allowing conjugal visits, and/or severely reducing custodial sentences especially in HIV vulnerable groups. Current policy of increasing custodial sentences whilst restricting public expenditure on prisons might be described as HIV friendly! Its epidemiological implications are terrifying.

(iv) *Control of Prostitution* – since prostitution involves not just those who are voluntary participants (clients and providers) but also their unwitting partners, it cannot altogether avoid public policy. Those who opposed the Contagious Diseases Acts of the nineteenth century did so mainly on the grounds that they conflicted with the individual rights of women and gave customers a false sense of security. Given the long incubation period of AIDS, similar Acts today might raise even stronger conflicts. Yet growing public pressure for State control of prostitution must be expected as AIDS spreads.

There are of course considerable difficulties in defining prostitution accurately – and it cannot be expected that any single public policy will be effective on every person who sells sexual intercourse to the public. Positive forms of control (e.g. financial inducements, parallel to the inducements sometimes used for those involved in food production, for HIV positive prostitutes to 'retire'), whilst being possibly effective on certain groups, might still conflict with the individual rights of some and again might foster a false security in others. Negative forms of control might take the form of tagging or enforced detention:

(v) *Tagging* – it might be possible to use some form of electronic tagging on those who are known to be HIV positive and yet who are still sexually active (or still actively sharing needles). The malicious, avaricious, psychotic or subnormal prostitute, drug user, or prisoner who knows himself or herself to be HIV positive and yet ignores advice, education or even financial inducements, may prompt active restraint by society in the interests of the common good – either by some form of electronic monitoring or possibly by some form of indelible mark visible to those intending to have sexual intercourse. Clearly this will severely conflict with the individual rights of those being restrained and may encourage others in a similar position to be more secretive and less inclined to be tested. And, again, it may give potential customers a false sense of security. Yet some form of tagging (if it could be made to work) might seem to be less ethically problematic than enforced detention.

(vi) *Enforced Detention* – this is already a possibility under the Public Health (Infectious Diseases) Regulations 1985, although it has so far very seldom been used. Clearly it would be very odd to propose incarceration as a serious policy option to control the spread of AIDS if the remarks on penal policy already made are taken seriously. However there may well be growing public demand in *Phase Three* that sexually active HIV positive prostitutes, 'enthusiastic amateurs', or drug abusers who do not respond to other inducements or sanctions, must be controlled by prisons or by secure isolation hospitals. Again, the long incubation period coupled with the incurability of AIDS faces this option with severe problems. Enforced detention would presumably have to be either for life or until the appropriate authorities were convinced that those involved had changed their sexual behaviour. However, the main ethical problem is that under this option the rights of the individual would be wholly subordinated to the well-being of society at large. This is not something that should be undertaken lightly.

(12) RECOMMENDATIONS

We are conscious of the need to make recommendations in this very vexed and problematic area of AIDS and Social Policy. It is our belief that ethically sustainable social action is required now. If such action is delayed further, then the public panic that may characterise *Phase Three* will, we suspect, encourage social policies which are not ethically sustainable. By acting decisively in advance of this panic some of the more egregious options may be avoided.

We recommend as follows:

(i) *Health Education*: We believe that the current stress upon condom use may be misleading epidemiologically and socially. Some of the literature we have seen apparently suggests that it is 'safe' for young people to have multiple sexual partners provided they use condoms. In contrast, we would like to see a much greater stress in health education upon 'healthy living'. Committed, long-term sexual relationships are a far 'safer' form of sexual behaviour than promiscuity relying upon condoms. This applies equally to heterosexual relationships and to homosexual relationships between men. Rather than promoting 'protection' based upon fear, we would like to see a more positive role being taken by health education. This would seek to promote the idea that it makes sense, epidemiologically and socially, to have sexual intercourse only within committed, long-term relationships, not within short-term and/or casual relationships. The latter are 'unhealthy' for a variety of serious medical reasons – not just AIDS, but also venereal diseases (which are increasing), cervical cancer, and infectious diseases generally. The arguments for 'healthy living' – or perhaps better 'healthy loving' – are every bit as powerful as those currently directed against smoking, drugs, obesity, or solvent abuse.

Although an emphasis upon 'healthy living' and upon committed, long-term relationships may be resisted by some sexual minority groups, it is important to remember that this is an issue which involves the whole community. The threat posed by the potential spread of AIDS requires a radical re-examination of sexual behaviour and attitudes in a culture in which influential voices have promoted sexual 'rights', without correlative 'duties', for so long. A stress simply upon condoms is wholly insufficient to counter this threat. Without resorting to what might be interpreted as partisan 'moralising', we believe that health education should be concerned to encourage 'healthy living' in this area, just as it already does in other areas.

(ii) *Health Promotion*: Even if the provision of condoms is seen as a 'second best' option, it nonetheless does still have a role to play in slowing down the spread of HIV infection. We believe that the provision of condoms in prisons should now become a routine procedure. Despite the conflicts with some concepts of punishment that this will undoubtedly cause, we believe that the arguments in favour of this provision are overwhelming.

(iii) *Information Gathering*: We believe that HIV infection should be treated on a par with other forms of contagious infection. As a result, we recommend that information gathering should be less cautious than it has been so far. We believe that there is a strong ethical case for implementing *non-anonymous, non-opt-out screening*, in at least certain specifiable situations (e.g. screening before surgery). Although this will mean some curtailment of what are often perceived to be individual rights, we believe that the rights of society at large, and indeed the common good, should in this instance be given priority. It is in the interests of the common good to have accurate information about the spread of this deadly infection, and for medical and nursing personnel to be warned about taking special (and, for surgeons, highly restrictive) precautions when treating those known to be carrying the virus. As *Phase Three* approaches, so we believe it will be right to remove present restrictions in this area.

(iv) *Contact Tracing*: We recognise that contact tracing also involves some infringement of individual rights, but here again we believe that the common good should take priority. Specifically, we believe that contact tracing should be introduced routinely on a par with contact tracing for other venereal infections.

(v) However, we are not persuaded that *notification* is a policy that should yet be implemented. Voluntary arrangements should be given longer to work. But again, especially as *Phase Three* approaches, it may be necessary to review the effectiveness of these arrangements. *Notification* would not seem to us to raise overwhelming ethical difficulties in the interests of the common good, especially when AIDS becomes widely prevalent.

(vi) *Penal Policy*: We believe that the attention of both Government and the Courts should be drawn to the need for an urgent reform of penal policy. Overcrowding in prisons, lack of conjugal visits, and an accelerating recourse to custodial sentences, all need to be questioned in the light of a likely spread of HIV infection. Much greater urgency, in what is already a problematic area, is required here.

(vii) *Control of Prostitution*: After reviewing the various options, we are not convinced that coercive attempts to control prostitutes will be either effective or ethically sustainable. Instead, much franker education is necessary here, both amongst women resorting to prostitution and amongst their potential customers. Attempts to make prostitution 'safer' - through regulated brothels, tagging, or enforced detention of those known to be infected – will we believe be counterproductive. They will effectively promote the idea that it is 'safe' to resort to legitimised prostitutes. In contrast, we would like to see a clear health education message to the effect that today prostitution is inherently unhealthy for all those who resort to it as well as for their sexual partners.

AIDS: Select Bibliography Consulted by all the Group

AIDS, HIV AND CIVIL LIBERTIES – Information for national conference held in Manchester Town Hall, 23–24 March 1990.

BLENDON, Robert and DONELAN, Karen – 'Discrimination against people with AIDS. The public's perspective'. Occasional Notes. *New England Journal of Medicine*, Vol 319, No. 15, 13 October 1988, pp. 1022–6.

BOND, Senga, RHODES, Tim, *et. al.* – A summary report of a national study of HIV infection, AIDS and community nursing staff in England, University of Newcastle upon Tyne, Health Care Research Unit, 1988.

CRISP, Roger – 'AIDS Symposium. Autonomy, welfare and the treatment of AIDS', *Journal of Medical Ethics*, 1989, 15, 68–73.

DEPARTMENT OF HEALTH – HC(88)40/HC(FP)(88)18/ LASSL(88)12, *AIDS (Control) Act 1987*, June 1988.

DEPARTMENT OF HEALTH – HC(88)66/HN(FP)(88)33, 'Resource distribution for 1988–90', December 1988.

ETHICS AND AIDS: a bibliography – *Bulletin of the Institute of Medical Ethics*, August 1988, pp. 13–24.

GILL, Liz – 'A testing war over AIDS', *The Times*, 3 November 1988.

GOLIBER, Thomas J. – 'Africa's expanding population: old problems, new policies', *Population Bulletin*, Vol. 44, No. 3, November 1989.

HASTINGS CENTER REPORT – *AIDS: the emerging ethical dilemmas*, Special Supplement, August 1985.

HASTINGS CENTER REPORT – *AIDS: public health and civil liberties*, Special Supplement, December 1986.

HAYRY, Heta and HAYRY, Matti – 'AIDS Now', *Bioethics*, Vol. 1, No. 4, 1987, pp. 339–56.

HIV, AIDS AND PRISONS – *Mainliners Newsletter*, Issue No. 2 – September 1990.

KAPILA, Mukesh – 'AIDS: a global perspective', *Health Promotion*, Vol. 3, No. 3, 1988, pp. 329–35.

MATTHEWS, G. W. and NESLUND, V. S. – 'The initial impact of AIDS on public health law in the United States – 1986', *Journal of the American Medical Association*, 1987, 257, pp. 344–52: and a review of the article in *Bulletin of the Institute of Medical Ethics*, June 1987, pp. 1–4.

MOHR, Richard D. – 'AIDS, Gays and State Coercion', *Bioethics*, Vol. 1, No. 1, 1987, pp. 35–50.

NATIONAL AIDS MANUAL – Section F8, Prisons.

NATIONAL ASSOCIATION OF PROBATION OFFICERS – Briefing. 'Sex, Drugs and Prison Walls'.

HOGG D. – 'No Condoms in Prison', Reported in *Mainliners Newsletter*, Issue No. 2 – September 1990.

NORTHERN REGIONAL HEALTH AUTHORITY – 'AIDS: A continuing threat to the public health', Report on the Health Service Response in the Northern Region, NRHA, 1988.

NORTHERN REGIONAL HEALTH AUTHORITY – 'Services for patients with HIV infection and AIDS in 1988/89, and deployment of AIDS allocation', April 1988.

OSBORN, June E. – 'AIDS: Politics and Science', Sounding Board, *New England Journal of Medicine*, Vol. 318, No. 7, 18 February 1988.

PEARL, David – 'AIDS: an overview of the legal implications', *The Law Society's Gazette*, No. 19, Wednesday 17 May 1989, pp. 28, 31 and 35.

PUBLIC HEALTH LABORATORY SERVICE – 'Communicable Disease Report. Acquired Immune Deficiency Syndrome in England and Wales to end 1993. Projections using data to end September 1989', Report of a Working Group convened by the Director of Public Health Laboratory Service.

SEX AND DRUGS AND PRISON WALLS – Letters from prisoners, *Mainliners Newsletter*, Issue No. 4 – November 1990.

UNITED KINGDOM HEALTH DEPARTMENTS and HEALTH EDUCATION AUTHORITY HIV and AIDS – 'An assessment of current and future spread in the UK', Proceedings of the Symposium held on Friday 24 November 1989, Queen Elizabeth II Conference Centre, Westminster, London, HEA/DoH/COI, 1990.

VAN HOOFT, Stan – Book Review of *AIDS and Public Policy*, edd. Christine Pierce and Donald Van De Veer, 1988, *Bioethics*, April 1989, pp. 171–4.

VARIETY OF HEALTH ADVICE LEAFLETS – leaflets on health advice issued in England and Scotland, 1989–90.

In Conclusion

A number of key ideas have guided this book. Christian values have been characterised as being intimately related to Christian communities. Since the Enlightenment, many thinkers have explored the idea that values can be derived from individual, rational thought, and from that alone. In contrast, I have argued that values are primarily carried in communities and are sustained over time by communities. And Christian values find their main basis in worshipping communities. However, in many societies Christian values have now spread beyond these worshipping communities. Furthermore, these Christian values may have deeply shaped the quality (but not necessarily the survival) of apparently secular worlds.

In this situation, Christian ethicists are in a privileged role. Their values are to be found scattered in what at first appear to be quite secular worlds. As a result opportunities for dialogue are still far more widespread than is often realised. Indeed, as many of those engaged in the sciences, medicine or the social sciences encounter new and morally perplexing dilemmas (as assuredly many of them do in an increasingly complex world), so they still turn to Christian ethicists – if they are available and willing to listen attentively.

Naturally in a pluralistic society there are others in all of these secular worlds who do not identify the dilemmas that they encounter as moral dilemmas. Business ethics, science ethics and (for fewer) medical ethics are for them non-subjects. They believe instead that all dilemmas are to be resolved pragmatically and that individuals in large organisations can never be held to be morally responsible for corporate issues. Others disagree. They believe in contrast that they are themselves responsible (however partially) even in large organisations and find it intolerable to pretend to be two different people, one at work and the other at home – Niebuhr's 'moral man and immoral society'.

On this understanding of Christian ethics an obvious tension soon arises once the discipline moves out into secular worlds. The Christian ethicist can work with an implicit or an explicit theology in these secular worlds. Some theologians believe that only explicit theology is legitimate. For them it is the duty of the Christian ethicist to proclaim to a secular world, to distinguish Christian values sharply from secular values, and to defend the alternative world that Christianity offers. As a result they believe that the primary task of Christian ethics is to present an internally coherent and theologically informed system of ethics – whatever the world at large thinks.

I believe that there are situations which require this approach to Christian ethics. The political and social context in Nazi Germany was so evil that a 'confessing church' option was indeed the proper one for Christian ethicists to adopt. A dialogue with the evils of Nazism would soon have drained any distinctive voice from Christian ethics. Yet I have tried to show in the course of this book that this is not the only, or even, in many secular worlds, the most appropriate way to do Christian ethics. In them a more implicit approach is required. Implicit theology is not a denial of theology, but rather a recognition that those working in secular (but not intrinsically evil) worlds often want patient guidance not sermons. It is also, I believe, a more pastorally sensitive approach to Christian ethics in secular worlds.

Naturally there are many issues unresolved in all of this. The next stage of my research must be more structural. It is all very well talking abstractly about 'worshipping communities', but the reality in Britain is that they are fast disappearing. If Christian values spill over from worshipping communities into society at large, over time they may become increasingly attenuated if their roots in these communities and the very communities themselves disappear.

Once a theory of secularisation would have been seen as a sufficient explanation of all of this. The demise of both Christian values in society at large and the worshipping communities that nurtured them were considered to be casualties of an ineluctable process of secularisation. In terms of this process, pragmatic means of dealing with dilemmas, which were once considered to be moral dilemmas, will eventually be the only ones generally available in a secularised society. Secularisation will have swept all but a small remnant before it. And Christian ethics will have become an esoteric activity for the socially marginal remnant of Christian sectarians that survive.

But it has already been noted that dissentient voices are being increasingly heard in the sociology of religion. The thorough-going secularisation thesis is no longer dominant. Instead the search has begun for other explanations of the decline charac-terising most British (but not American) churches. In my next book, *The Myth of the Empty Church*, I will attempt to show how attention to the previously uncorrelated mass of longi-tudinal census data on churchgoing offers alternative explana-tions. It also contains, I will argue, radical implications for institutional churches and for the effective (and, for me person-ally, essential) survival of worshipping communities.

Beyond that I must return to the theoretical issues for Christian ethics raised in this book. I hope to do this in an extended study of *Moral Communities*. The full implications of the challenge presented by Alasdair MacIntyre and others have yet to be unpacked.

All of this is for the future. For the present it is perhaps sufficient to stress that doing Christian ethics in secular worlds is a worthwhile and rewarding activity. It is worthwhile because it is an activity which crosses disciplines and boundaries and engages minds beyond a narrow theological elite. And it is rewarding because it promises discoveries yet to be made.

Index